PEACOCK BASS ADDICTION

12 Steps To Survive The Jubilation and Ecstasy!

by Larry Larsen

Eight-Time World Record Holder and
1999 Inductee in Fishing Hall of Fame

Larsen's Outdoor Publishing

This Book Courtesy of:

Copyright (c) 1999 by Larry Larsen

Publisher's Cataloging in Publication

Larsen, Larry.
  Peacock bass addiction: 12 steps to survive the jubilation and ecstasy!   by Larry Larsen.

  p. cm.
  Includes index.
  ISBN 0-936513-49-7

  1. Bass fishing.   2. Peacock bass.   I. Title.   II. Title: Peacock bass addiction.

SH681.L37 1999   799.1'78

ISBN 0-936513-49-7
Library of Congress 99-94024

Published by:
LARSEN'S OUTDOOR PUBLISHING
2640 Elizabeth Place, Lakeland, FL 33813
(941) 644-3381   fax (941) 644-3288

PRINTED IN THE UNITED STATES OF AMERICA

1 2 3 4 5 6 7 8 9 10

LIBRARY ANNOTATION

Title: Peacock Bass Addiction

Author: Larry Larsen
Publisher: Larsen's Outdoor Publishing
Copyright: 1999

Sports & Recreation
Fishing
799.1

LCCN: 99-94024
ISBN: 0-936513-49-7

ADULT SMALL PRESS

From a Fishing Hall of Fame Legendary Angler and outdoors journalist, "Peacock Bass Addiction" focuses on catching America's greatest gamefish, the peacock bass. It offers tips on where, when and how to catch the exciting fish. Special features include range/seasonal movements, tackle, fly fishing, battle tips and top locations in the world.

192 pages
Paperbound/Casebound

Table of Contents
Index
B&W Illustrations
Photographs

** Author Credentials **
He's America's most widely-read bass fishing writer and author. More than 1,800 of Larsen's articles have appeared in magazines, including Outdoor Life, Florida Sportsman, Sports Afield, Bassin' and Field & Stream. He was inducted into the Fishing Hall of Fame in 1999. Larsen has authored 19 books on bass fishing and contributed chapters to another eight.

DEDICATION

This book is dedicated to those who have tossed a plug in search of a monster known as the peacock bass, and who then became addicted to them; those of us that are in a seemingly endless spiral to chase the monster forever, to all wet corners of the earth, until we have caught the biggest, the baddest, and the best of their specie. It is also dedicated to the peacock bass "novice" with a yearning to become addicted to this fish. If you can't say no to a trip into the jungle after peacock bass, you will become addicted. That's guaranteed. This is dedicated to those avid "tough" fish anglers who chase musky, king salmon, huge pike and other species growing into triple digit weights, who have been brought to their knees by a monstrous, full-grown, belligerent peacock bass. Enjoy!

ACKNOWLEDGMENTS

Again, I want to thank my friends in the outdoor travel industry, those tour operators, trip outfitters and tourism people that offer some of the most exciting, adventuresome opportunities in the world. A list of many of the helpful contacts who provided assistance and advice to make this effort comprehensive and interesting would have to include: Dick Ballard, Angling Adventures; J.W. Smith, Rod & Gun; Ron Speed Jr., Adventures; Scott Swanson, Quest; Howard McKinney, Fishabout; Phil Marsteller, Amazon Tours; Dr. Jan Wilt, Ecotur Park, Luis Brown, River Plate Outfitters; Carlos Arroyo, Thaimacu Lodge; Russ Clement, Xingu Lodge; Christine Serrao, ParaTur; and Frank Ibarra, Manaka Lodge.

Special thanks also to guides Rodolfo Fernandez, John Jardin and Alan Zaremba, taxidermist Don Frank, Florida fisheries biologist Paul Shafland, Gary King of Outdoor Technologies Group, Ken Syphrett, Phil Jensen of Luhr-Jensen Lures, Ken Chaumont of Bill Lewis Lures, and my many other friends in the tackle industry. I also wish to thank Ricardo Freire of FEIPESCA for his support in presenting seminars to thousands of Brazilians at the huge fishing Expo in Sao Paulo, and to Andy Hahn who translated my first peacock book, "Peacock Bass Explosions" into Portuguese for the Brazilian version, "O Explosivo Tucunare!".

I owe a special debt of gratitude to my very good friend and renown angler, Homer Circle, and to the National Fresh Water Fishing Hall of Fame Board for considering me worthy of election as a "Legendary Angler." I am deeply honored by my induction.

PREFACE

Angling for the exciting peacock bass is rapidly growing in popularity. Anglers quickly become addicted to this specie, whose native range is the Amazon jungles of South America. The focus of this book, "Peacock Bass Addiction" is how, where, and when to catch the great sport fish.

Effective tactics and secret techniques to fool the provocative fish are presented throughout the book. Detailed illustrations and numerous photos highlight the most productive lures and patterns. The book is a valuable reference source with numerous strategies in each chapter to fool peacock bass. Many of the proven techniques discussed are applicable to waters around the world.

This is a how-to book designed to help you catch more peacock bass, and it is more. It attempts to provide readers with an honest overview of numerous opportunities in South America and around the world where peacock bass exist. Each of the first 12 chapters in this comprehensive book focuses on geographic areas in the various countries that almost always produce good peacock bass fishing. Some of those also reveal other exciting species that are found in the same waters. Dorado, payara, pacu, and red-tail catfish are among the species highlighted in the text.

Chapter 13, "Battles Won and Lost", provides an experienced viewpoint on how to win battles with the giants. It points out common ways to lose the fish of your dreams and ways to prevent such a catastrophe. Chapter 14 discusses the range and seasonal movements of the peacock bass, critical elements to the success of any venture.

The rainy season and dry season effects on the resource is unique to the Amazonas Region of South America. Knowing the critical water conditions should prevent an angler from making a major mistake in timing. Most readers will highly value the seasonal calendar shown.

I am often asked about the most appropriate tackle to carry along on an expedition. In Chapter 15, I discuss my favorite lures, tackle, and types of habitat to use them in. Detailed in Chapter 16 is fly fishing advice from experts on catching peacocks using their top flies. Readers will discover several interesting and informative appendices, including detailed information on the first and second books in this series, "Peacock Bass Explosions" and "Peacock Bass & Other Fierce Exotics" respectively, and an Outdoor Resource Directory.

CONTENTS

The author and his favorite bass have been featured on the covers of many magazines in the U.S. and in South America. Larry has sold articles and photos of peacock bass to Sports Afield, Outdoor Life and many other magazines, brochures and internet sites.

Larry Larsen's "Peacock Bass Explosions" book has been translated into Portuguese and published in Brazil by a huge publishing conglomerate. His first two peacock bass books, in English, are outlined in the Appendix

ABOUT THE AUTHOR

Larry Larsen is America's most widely read and respected bass fishing writer and author and is the only one to pen three books on peacock bass. He is a frequent contributor on both largemouth and peacock bass subjects to major outdoor magazines, including *Sports Afield, Field & Stream, Bassin', Outdoor Life,* and *Florida Sportsman.* His photography and articles have appeared in more than 1,800 magazines.

The renown angler has caught and released hundreds of peacock bass between five and 23 pounds and has traveled hundreds of thousands of miles to fish for peacock bass, including stops in Brazil, Peru, Colombia, Venezuela, Panama, Costa Rica and Hawaii. In 1999, Larsen was inducted into the National Fresh Water Fishing Hall of Fame as a Legendary Angler.

Larsen is a seven-time world line class record holder on the peacock bass and an all-tackle, IGFA world record holder for a 10 pound, 8 ounce butterfly peacock. The IGFA record fish (cichla ocellaris) peacock was taken on a Luhr-Jensen Big Game Woodchopper in a lagoon off the Rio Branco in the Brazilian state of Roraima.

"A small float plane dropped off my Indian guide, Ivon, and I on a tiny creek in the middle of the Amazon Rain Forest," says Larsen. "We had a 10-foot PortaBoat and 5 hp outboard to traverse 40 miles of totally unexplored water in the following two days. We found one small lagoon with several giant butterflies, and I caught the record after landing two others in the 8 to 9 pound class within 20 feet of each other. In my 25 or so trips to the Amazon, I have never found concentrations of large butterflies weighing more than five or six pounds."

He was awarded line class world records in '93, '94 and '95 for speckled peacock bass (Cichla spp) by the National Fresh Water Fishing Hall of Fame in Hayward, WI. The records for the seven peacock bass, which weighed up to 20 pounds, were established in the 6, 14, 16, 17, 20 and unlimited pound line classes. He has also caught payara and Silver Croaker in South American waters which qualified as all-tackle world records.

It is improbable that readers would not learn something from Larry's knowledge and experience with peacock bass. There are no journalists more qualified or knowledgeable about such waters. In fact, only a couple of anglers in the world have fished as many areas and caught as many giant peacock bass as Larry. Those who study these pages will expand their knowledge of the addiction that is called "peacock bass fishing."

The author/angler intensely studies all aspects of a fishing topic before writing about it. His works detail the proven fish locating and catching techniques. Larsen has worked with several tackle companies on lure development, drawing on his many years of fishing experience and an engineering background. He has fished bass extensively for more than 38 years, and for peacock bass more than 10 years.

The Lakeland, Florida outdoor writer/photographer has now authored 19 award-winning books on bass fishing and contributed chapters to another eight. They include the BASS SERIES LIBRARY, the GUIDE TO FLORIDA BASS WATERS SERIES, "LARSEN ON BASS TACTICS", and others. They also include the other two books in the PEACOCK BASS SERIES, "Peacock Bass Explosions" and "Peacock Bass & Other Fierce Exotics". They are available from the author (see Resource Directory in back of this book). He has also authored books on saltwater fishing opportunities in Florida and the Caribbean.

Larsen is also President of Larsen's Outdoor Publishing (LOP), publishing a variety of outdoor titles, and a member of the Outdoor Writers Association of America (OWAA), the Southeastern Outdoor Press Association (SEOPA), and the Florida Outdoor Writers Association (FOWA). Complete information on the author's other books and the LOP line of outdoor books can be found in the Resource Directory at the back of this book.

INTRODUCTION - PEACOCK BASS ADDICTION

12-step program for conventional anglers, the foot-long-plug tossers and even the fly guys!

"Peacock Bass euphoria is when your adrenalin and your mind are working overtime attempting to compensate for your physical strength and endurance which are shot."--Larry Larsen, 1999

My arms were shaking so hard I had to lay my rod down. My chest was heaving as I grasped at short breaths. Sweat poured from my brow and every other part of my body, and I felt faint from the jubilation. I had just become addicted. The 16-pounder lay at my feet with the small red and white Jerkin' Sam securely affixed to its jaw. After a couple of hundred small to mid-size peacock bass, I had finally captured a "teener". One that was truly a monster. A giant. A behemoth. Such monikers pale with the experience of controlling and capturing such a fish.

Glee turned to an uncontrollable laugh as I reached for a can of coke. My guide, a small Indian with dark eyes and few teeth, smiled. He knew the symptoms. He had guided gringos to the euphoric state before.

I had to have more. I regained as much composure as I could and started tossing my bait again to the flooded forest with reckless abandon. My first cast back to the vicinity of my big fish strike tangled in a fallen tree. I popped it free, and the guide ducked as my lure slammed into the side of our aluminum boat. My second, adrenaline-induced effort was off target as well, wrapping around a tree limb about 20 feet above my newly found honey hole.

It was a sign, I felt, to just slow down. I had to keep the adrenalin in check if I was to assume my normally very accurate casting and effective fishing. I did slow down that afternoon, but fishing for giant peacock bass was in my blood, forever. It was flowing in my veins through my heart.

There were no more giants for me that week on Lake Guri, only countless numbers of fish 3 to 11 pounds. But this was only my second trip to South America to experience the hardest hitting, fiercest-fighting fish in the world. I had to have more. I could not live without it. I was addicted to this South American siren, and today, I realize there is little I can do about it.

I've said it before, and I'll say it again. And again. And again. The peacock bass is a super aggressive fish with a downright belligerent personality. It is so powerful that it can destroy tackle and straighten hooks. The exciting fish will smash and tangle lures and even break them apart. If the lure's trebles have not been torn loose from the plug, the peacock bass will then give you the battle of your life.

It is impossible to exaggerate the ferocity and impact of their surface strike and the incredible fight of this colorful gamefish. You have to anticipate their violent strikes. Watch their "V" wake accelerate behind your erratically-retrieved bait, as you anticipate a blasting strike. The peacock may knock the plug into the air and then "field" it as it falls back to the surface.

The fish almost always jumps the second it is hooked, and after a head-shaking leap or three will make an unbelievable run. I have witnessed the total destruction of numerous well-constructed bass lures more times than I wish, and all of that carnage supported their unequaled reputation and fed my addiction.

The fact that they school with other fish of similar size leads to their being easily triggered into a feeding frenzy. Their competitive spirit is higher than any other fish that I know of. A partner who is quick and accurate can pitch a lure to the same area of a hooked fish or where a strike occurred and elicit the same results, an instant hookup.

Jim Chapralis, Editor of The PanAngler newsletter, calls us "obsessed", willing to fish dangerous areas and endure numerous hardships for a shot at a giant peacock bass. I contend that is not an obsession but an addiction.

In fact, Chapralis calls the growing number of dedicated fishermen who fish South America's jungles for peacock bass "a developing cult". For many, he says, it's "a way of life." I can't argue that, but it is more. It is not simply dedication; it's addiction.

It is an uncontrollable craving which develops into a psychological dependence for catching giant peacock bass. The angler acquires greater tolerance for the fish and therefore requires more and more trips in search of peacock action. Should this supply ever be cut off, the angler will suffer extreme "withdrawal" symptoms which are psychologically grueling.

☒ Two Dozen Checks To Verify Addiction

1. Knows that 4/0 4X hooks are much stronger than 4/0 3X hooks.
2. Is awake at 5 a.m. and asleep at 9 p.m.
3. Is willing to travel all night long arriving "brain dead" at the destination waters.
4. Has cut up thumbs, finger blisters and torn gloves.
5. Carries three or four extra rods and reels in the event the primary three break.
6. Has a tackle box full of lures, all over 6 inches in length.
7. Has frequent flyer accounts on airlines with names like Varig, LAB, Aeropostal, Vasp, Aeroperu and Transbrazil.
8. Has available bulk spools of 60 to 100 pound test braid.
9. Possesses worn-out copies of the two books, "Peacock Bass Explosions" and "Peacock Bass & Other Fierce Exotics".
10. Wears "Peacock Bass Explosions" T-shirt with color renditions of 7 species and subspecies ... to bed.
11. Has a replica of the angler's largest peacock bass in his living room.
12. Carries a pair of split ring pliers.
13. Is accustomed to fishing in lightweight long pants and long sleeve shirts, and long bill, wide-brim hat or cap.
14. Aging painfully but happily due to battles with big fish.
15. Frequently has tickets with travel routed through Miami.
16. Has healthy supply of anti-diarrhea pills.
17. Has more photos of 20 plus pound peacock bass in the wallet than of children and grandchildren.
18. Values a hook sharpener more in the travel bag than a toothbrush.
19. Sells bass boat and doesn't fish frequently for black bass like he did before.
20. Packs a rod tube for a 7 to 9 day "business" trip.
21. Buys home-study Portuguese language tapes to learn how to say "Let's go fishing."
22. Flies with three other 230-plus pound strangers in four-person, single engine float plane with doubtful maintenance schedule to land in unknown river channels.
23. Flies with three other 230-plus pound strangers in four-person, single engine wheel aircraft with doubtful maintenance schedule to land on machete-carved, one-lane dirt strip in the rainforest.
24. Visits places where the nearest phone is 300 miles away

The 12 Step Program

Finding a living peacock bass addict who no longer chases his quarry is almost impossible. Therefore, help from a "recovered" individual in controlling an addict is hard to find. Peacock bass addicts passing along their stories is what gets newcomers in similar straits. Intervention through friends or relatives may help, but certainly only the individual can determine whether or not he or she is addicted and whether they can "recover."

Even monster peacock bass school with other fish of similar size. While Larry's guide admires this 20-pounder just landed, the addict's lure is again "wet" in hopes of enticing another giant.

My suggested program of "recovery" follows as the 12 Step Program. Here it is:

1. Admit you are powerless over peacock bass fishing video, audio, and print media information. Just be informed by thoroughly reading all three of the existing Peacock Bass Library of books: "Peacock Bass Explosions", "Peacock Bass & Other Fierce Exotics", and this one, "Peacock Bass Addiction".

2. Have confidence that a series of bad-weather trips can help restore your sanity. The water level and fishery production cannot be optimal in all cases. Agents that don't call off high water trips can provide some relief from your addiction.

3. Make out your will and leave all tackle to charity. Not knowing the optimal use of such gear, the charity's chances of becoming addicted are minimal.

4. Take an inventory of your oversized peacock bass tackle. Determine a reorder schedule for receiving an amply supply of the giant baits two months before your next trip.

5. Admit to all, including yourself, the exact nature of your addiction. Show them copies of your peacock bass books and your photo album.

6. Be ready to lose lures, rods and reels, and baggage. Plan on taking extra tackle including line, and don't pack a suitcase with anything you can't live without.

7. Humbly, go fishing for largemouth bass, snook, and even panfish. Limit half your tackle to the less-addictive species that lie closer to your home.

8. Make a list of all domestic chores we have skipped out on and make amends to those affected by such decisions. Why not take them peacock bass fishing to that "hot", can't miss location?

9. When we have harmed others by our addiction, admit promptly the wrongdoing. Invite along only fishing partners who truly can afford the trips and afford joining you in your addiction.

10. Seek out further knowledge of peacock bass fishing opportunities and have the power to overlook some. Select only those uniquely situated to provide great numbers of the quarry in all size year-classes from fingerlings to giants.

11. Practice total catch-and-release for thoughtful conservation of the species, and exercise minimal fishing pressures on the delicate resources. Handle trophy fish minimally to avoid their being overstressed.

12. As a result of these steps, carry this message to others and continue to practice the principles. Also, invest wisely in mutual funds.

New addicts that are not willing to or are unable to follow the 12 Step Program in its entirety should not worry. This addiction is progressive, however, and cannot be cured in the ordinary sense of the term. It can be arrested by total abstinence from peacock bass fishing, but the "hooked" angler will more likely need books, videos, magazines and a support group. The addict will likely need bandages, pain killer, gloves, belt, elastic bandage, sport cream, etc., as he or she continues to chase the "dream of this ecstasy".

Yes, this addiction can lead to a variety of injuries, and I have had them all. I recently sprained (or jammed) my thumb on a tremendous strike from a giant peacock bass. The last time that I had a sprained thumb was while playing basketball in high school over 35 years ago! Following the 12 Steps may help eliminate some of the uncomfortable symptoms of the addictions.

What This Addiction Is All About

The root of the problem is that the peacock is not really a "bass" at all. The peacock and the black bass, similar in stature and sporting qualities, are genetically far apart. The peacock, which has attained documented weights of 27 pounds, is called bass because it strongly resembles a largemouth in general size and shape. However, it is actually the largest American member of the cichlid family of fishes which also includes the guapote, oscar, and tilapia, among many others.

The cichlid family, with 1,400 species in the world and 250 to 300 in South America, is to tropical waters what the sunfish family, which includes the black basses, is to temperate freshwaters of North America. The IGFA and National Fresh Water Fishing Hall of Fame do recognize the fish under the common name of peacock bass, but the bucket-mouth peacock is more commonly called "pavon" in most Spanish-speaking countries and "tucunare" in Brazil, Peru and Hawaii.

Once you see the fish, you'll understand why it is called a peacock bass by most North Americans. The peacock bass derivesits name from the large conspicuous, ocellated (ringed in gold)black mark on its tail, which resembles the vivid "eye" on the beautiful plume of a peacock's tail. Hence the name, "peacock bass." The distinctive gold-embroidered circular black halo spot on all peacock bass tails reminds some more of the savage eye of a jungle cat.

The prominent "false eye" on the tail is actually a deceptive target for predators. Most all fish have a black eye on their heads, and some have evolved physically one or two ways to "misguide" an attack to the eye area from predators. One common evolution is the eye spot near the rear of the fish.

Another is vivid and irregular color patterns on the head and body that obscure the eye and detract from its prominence.

The Tempting Thugs

While peacock bass are similar to largemouth in many ways, they are tougher, meaner and bigger. Their strength seems impossible for a fish even twice their size. Peacock bass seldom find a menu item they don't like and after dark, they sleep a full night. As a result, they feed voraciously, but only during daylight hours.

Peacock bass are "demons" that are not affected by the moon; I have had tremendous fishing days on full moons and then equally great days two weeks later on a quarter moon.

The peacock bass being something of a thug is a real challenge. Many fish roam in schools, but the peacock bass is known for roaming in gangs. A hooked fish triggers the others in the school to search and destroy prey of their own. Leaving a hooked fish in the water until a second one nearby is hooked may prolong the excitement.

Their ferocious reputation for violent blasts of lures inspired my first book on the species. These addictive strikes may occur the instant the lure lands or they may occur the instant the lure is lifted from the water at boatside. At times, two or more peacocks may go after the same lure or even two casts to the same general area.

Most of the real giant peacock bass are taken in countries that have some currency that may not be worth a lot. But the real treasure in places like Brazil and Venezuela is in their peacock bass waters. There, monster peacocks are an addiction that few North American anglers can resist. Most addicts release the giants to once again have an opportunity for the ultimate battle.

Peacock "doubles" by two anglers are fairly common, as is catching two very competitive fish on the same plug. A seductive lure often triggers a race for it. Most addicts have had this experience.

My fishing partners know that I like to use a "team" approach to catching peacocks. Either of us is allowed, make that requested, to toss a lure toward any sign of a fish, strike or hook-up. A quick and accurate caster can increase hook-ups two-fold sometimes. On one occasion, lure maker Sam Griffin and I had 12 doubles in one day. And, we each had more single hook-ups than that.

Luring us further into the addiction is the fact that the peacock has extremely powerful jaws that can destroy lures and egos. A strong hook

A monster butterfly peacock can only feed an angler's "addiction". Here, the guide hefts Larry's IGFA All-Tackle World Record butterfly, which weighed 10 pounds, 8 ounces on certified scales.

set is required to drive the steel into their bony mouth, so the hooks should be needle-sharp. In fact, an addict's paraphernalia should always include a hone sharpener.

You'll have a battle "royale" on your hands from the minute a peacock slams the bait and rips off several yards of line, if it can. It is probably best to set the drag for a 20-pounder and not try to adjust the drag during the fight. The fish will jump frequently and rattle their gills in an exciting display power and control. Don't count the battle over until the fish is landed. And remember, both of you have been "hooked."

The Booking "Junkies"

The conduit to this addiction are the booking agents who make the fish so accessible and the trip so attractive. Not all opportunities are as good as they look in a video or brochure. As an addict, know what you want in a trip.

The author has traveled with most of the reputable booking agents (and a couple not so). Even though the vast majority are very honest in their assessment of the fishing conditions, risk and expected catches, peacocks like Larry's 19-pounder here, focus the brain on one thing and contribute to the addiction.

As with an addiction, danger may be present in some cases. There is a risk when traveling in the third world, especially to very remote areas that may offer the very best fishing. Some areas are more risky or dangerous than others, so it is up to the individual traveler to determine what is most acceptable to him. There may be political problems to deal with, and some fishing areas in Colombia and along its borders are dangerous.

Erland von Sneidern's Orinoco Ark on the Matavani River in Colombia was the first peacock bass operation many, many years ago, but after a couple of his houseboats were sunk, he built El Morichal Lodge near a military base at Puerto Carreno. Still, some interests in the rainforest of that country didn't want his clients boating around the secluded tributaries far from civilization. They kidnaped him and 75 days later, his brother and cousin rescued him in a deadly shootout. He then closed down all operations there.

Most of the sportfishing for peacock today takes place in Brazil, Venezuela and Peru. There are no guarantees on safety, although almost all of the current operators offer very safe trips. Certain countries have more than their share of problems, and as a result, few outfitters will offer Americans trip packages into questionable areas.

Some trips offer large numbers of peacock while others offer a chance a some giants and few little ones. Some outfitters have options in between and others may offer a variety of species of exotic fish. Some fishing trips emphasize the "ecotourism" aspects while others are focused squarely on hard-core anglers. Some trips are very comfortable and service is top-notch, while others are "rough" with minimal comforts. Some trips offer easy access and other are a logistical nightmare. Most can be addictive, but not all are addictive to all addicts.

I have, in penning this effort, assumed that most readers have read and studied my first two books on peacock bass. The information presented herein adds to that compendium of knowledge. For ease of reference, I have taken the liberty of mentioning in many chapters following some of the specific chapters in "Peacock Bass Explosions" and "Peacock Bass & Other Fierce Exotics" that will add to the overall knowledge of a local, operation, or how-to lore to better inform the addict to peacock bass fishing.

Chapter 1

RUMBLE IN THE RORAIMA JUNGLE

Aggression Disorder In The Agua Boa Watershed

My Indian guide directed our flat-bottom aluminum boat towards the swampy waters in the back of a small lagoon off the river. He grabbed a machete and moved past me to start whittling at a jungle of vines and brush. Five minutes later, he had cut down enough wood branches to squeeze our craft into a small, undefined creek with less dense obstacles.

As he whacked off the limbs and vines, I grabbed various tree branches and pushed our boat forward. I marveled at numerous wild orchids growing in the treetops amidst huge philodendrons whose roots stretched downward like tendrils. My guide, Cinval Gutierre, cut through the maze of several small trees with huge balls of bugs or "piones" clinging to their bark. The fifteen minutes of intense exercise in the equatorial sun, although under a partially-shaded canopy of forest, proved to be worth it. A small ten acre lagoon opened in front of us. Later, I affectionately named the lagoon "Lago de Larry".

As Cinval slowly paddled away from the dense perimeter, he pointed to a subtle dimple on the surface of the lagoon about 40 feet out. I lofted my Big Game Woodchopper toward the spot and it splashed down on target. My initial twitch of the bait garnered an explosion from the territorial monster who then went ballistic. A powerful run punctuated by intermittent aerobatics revealed a giant, very upset fish.

The spool of braid on my Abu-Garcia Morrum shrunk to about half its former size as the awesome peacock charged toward the far side of the small lake. The belligerent fish finally slowed down and turned as I gained a modicum of control with the baitcaster. After two more spectacular jumps, the fish's heaving gills was a sign it was tiring. My

Larry caught this 19-pound peacock in the mouth of one of the lagoons off the Agua Boa River.

outfit's smooth drag and steady rod pressure finally brought the big boy to the boat.

Cinval grabbed the giant tail and hauled it aboard. We quickly weighed and measured the peacock and then released it to swim back toward the depths. The 19 pounder was 32 1/2 inches long and almost 20 inches in girth. The stout fish waved goodbye with its broad tail as it slapped a face-full of water over the gunwale onto my guide.

We laughed, and at the same time a boiling melee offshore further down the bank caught our attention. Three or four giant fish were gorging on smaller baitfish a very long cast away. I stood up and sent my plug to the edge of the activity and braced for what I knew would come. I was not disappointed.

A peacock bass larger than the previous one exploded on my bait and tried again to stretch my 60-pound test Trilene braid. The fish smoked away burning a new "life line" into my palm. It headed perpendicular to my pulls toward the protective confines of submerged trees nearer shore. He made it. I cried.

I picked up another outfit with a big Super Trap tied on and cast it to area of original interest. Three cranks later, a 13-pounder tried to make off with it. I whipped that fish and released it, but the one I really wanted was swimming free. Oh, well. The 19 pounder was the largest peacock taken that week on my visit to the Rio Agua Boa, which may be the world's best peacock bass waters.

I was fishing the lagoons of the small blackwater tributary lying west of the turbid Rio Branco in the most northern part of Brazil. Missouri anglers Don McCann, Shawn Patrick, Larry Sherwood and tour booking agent Dick Ballard had traveled with me to the Ecotur Park Lodge, our base. We had all done well. I had caught about 15 peacock bass in the teens and the other anglers had several as well. On small Lago Mendosa on just one morning Sherwood and I caught 50 bass that averaged 8 pounds each. It's interesting to note that was the same walk-in lake where I had found little activity just 8 months earlier on a previous trip.

Aggression Beyond Belief

This time, the fish were so active it was relatively easy to catch and release 25 to 30 peacocks per day per person in these secluded waters of the Rain Forest. The average weight was significant, around 8 pounds. On one occasion, I caught a 15 pounder while Sherwood hooked and landed an 11 pounder at the same time. I personally had at least 30 strikes right at the boat with no more than one foot of line off the rod tip.

On another occasion, I had reeled in a minnow bait fouled with weeds. I held the Series One graphite in my left hand while using my right to pull weeds off the lure. Then, I tossed the weed-free plug over the side, and started to move the rod from my left hand to my right to ready another cast. When the lure hit the water, however, a 10 1/2 pounder exploded on it, almost jerking the 7-foot, medium-heavy action rod from my hands. It tore off 30 feet of my 60 pound test line before I gained control and fought it back to the boat.

You know the peacock bass are aggressive when they grab your line in front of the lure and then swim off for 15 feet or so before releasing it. One did just that, and I had numerous strikes at my line. One peacock even chased along the surface that point where my line entered the water. His v-wake right behind that moving point was well in front of my lure.

I caught four types of peacock in the waters of the Agua Boa: the "paca" or speckled, the "acu" (pronounced assu) or grande, the "balinha" (pronounced balleia) or butterfly and the "toua" (pronounced tawah) which is a small peacock with maximum weight of 2 pounds and one without any side markings - bars, dashes, or rosettes. I also caught other species such as paiche cashorro (a barracuda-like fish), bicuda (with a beak), black and silver piranha, and arawana (a long, thin fish with a

The Rio Agua Boa has many peacocks in the 12 to 17 pound range. Trip agent Dick Ballard shows off a typical "teener."

continuous fin from its dorsal to its pectoral). I also caught a freshwater stingray, which after Cinval's handiwork with the machete, I called "Stubby".

The water level that November was slightly higher than normal and it rose 3 to 4 feet during the week I was there. That rise seemed to move the fish in the connected lagoons to deeper hideouts. The peacocks slammed our topwater plugs early in the week, and then submerged baits, such as the Luhr-Jensen #18 Pet Spoon and the Bill Lewis Super Trap, became more effective later on.

Pack-In Escapes

The lagoons and "resacas", or oxbow lakes, off the Agua Boa are all surrounded by a variety of hardwoods, including mahogany and palm trees. Bright yellow and orange bushes color the shoreline further. The 66-mile long river borders the Roraima State Ecological Park for 40

Anglers ready their gear to chase after giant peacock. Boats are always ready at Ecotur Park Lodge, a very comfortable facility with an adjacent landing trip carved into the Amazon Rain Forest.

miles or so and is about two casts wide for most of its run. The river headwaters are in the Serra da Mocidade mountains near the Yanomami Indian Territory southwest of Boa Vista. One can see the mountain peaks which rise to over 6,000 feet from the fishing grounds north of the lodge.

The Agua Boa has numerous white sand bars on the inner bends where alligators and thirsty animals can be seen, but most of the giant peacock bass are in the lagoons. There are 12 productive resacas within a 1 1/2 hour boat ride of the lodge. Most are between 8 and 16 acres and generally have visibilities of 7 to 10 feet.

"They vary in depth from 3 to 15 feet," explains Ballard who has fished the waters more than any other American. "There are 8 other clear-water lakes connected by small canals or creeks off the Agua Boa that are similar in size and depth. All hold big populations of peacock bass, and some now exceed 20 pounds."

The 15 land-lock lakes require a short walk of from two minutes to the closest, to maybe 20 for the most distant. The paths are along well marked trails through an impressive array of tropical flora. A botanical garden of sorts, the cleared walkways meander through bogs, fallen timber and an immense variety of trees and plants. Plate-sized orchids of various colors and other air plants cling to partially-balding trees while masses of aerial roots cascade from lush canopies of large banyon-type trees. Fortunately, the "hike" is an easy jaunt to productive waters with absolutely no pressure.

On the river and resacas, 16-foot aluminum boats equipped with 25 horsepower outboards, electric trolling motors and swivel seats are used; the same boats are stationed on the land-locked lagoons. An angler only

Dr. Jan Wilt, developer of the Ecotur Park Lodge, is an avid angler who has caught lots of giant peacock.

has to transfer his fishing gear overland to the boat, while the guide will portage the battery and trolling motor and/or paddle and cooler.

Wild Beginnings

On my first trip to the lodge, fishing partner Ballard and I were traveling with angling guests John Atchley of Jupiter, Florida and Georgians Chris Parker and George Johnson. Dr. Jan Wilt, Director of Ecotur Park, was our host. The European-born physician and owner of a hospital in the Roraima state's largest city, Boa Vista, is the developer of the Ecotur Park Lodge where we stayed in the seclusion of the Rain Forest.

Dr. Wilt is a gregarious man who speaks broken English, in addition to his fluency in three other languages. He is an avid angler and his knowledge is addictive. Dick and I followed our host and his boat to a nearby lagoon that afternoon where the doctor's angling proficiency was quickly evidenced. Within 20 minutes, he headed toward us to show us his catch. He held up a 13 1/2 pound peacock for us to admire and photograph. We watched him release the big fish and began casting with

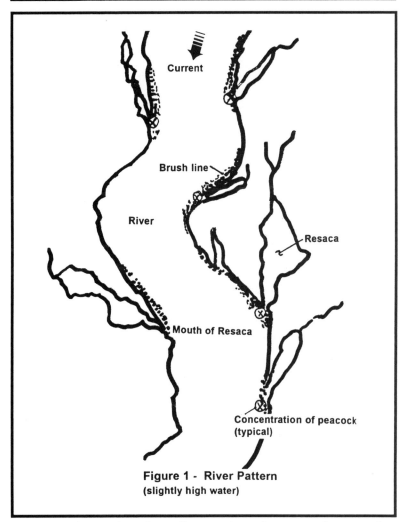

Figure 1 - River Pattern
(slightly high water)

Figure 1 - The Rio Aqua Boa offers two dozen lagoons with outstanding low-water peacock bass fishing. When the water is only slightly high, the "river pattern" comes into its own. On a trip to these waters last year, Dick Ballard discovered that fishing the mouths of very tiny resacas with some inundated bushes acting as a river buffer can yield great catches. Simply working the river, moving from one resaca to another, can result in very big fish in large numbers. The peacock concentrations are located in the quiet waters just behind the bush "frontage".

renewed enthusiasm. Dick and I took about 30 peacock up to 9 1/2 pounds on that first afternoon in Dr. Wilt's favorite lake.

That's a very respectable catch for our initial efforts, but the fishing the rest of the week got even better. The following morning, I tossed large Big Game Woodchoppers and Dick smaller, hard plastic minnow baits on Lago Castahho to amass 60 peacocks. We caught and released five peacocks weighing between 10 and 12 1/2 pounds along its productive flats and its tiny back lake.

After a slower afternoon, my partner and I caught 45 the next morning, including the largest of our trip, my 14 pounder. The big fish caught in Lago Braulino (Lago de Larry) measured 30 inches in length and 19 inches in girth.

Name Change Waters

Dick and I caught 75 peacock bass the following day and the size was impressive. That morning, we went into Lago Serrinha, which we quickly nick-named "10-pound lake" because of its abundance of fish in the 10 to 11 pound range. About 18 of our 40 peacock taken in the three hours weighed exactly 10 pounds. We lost several that would have also been that weight and the others caught and released that morning averaged around 8 pounds each. When I returned to the same lake on my second trip, I had to rename it. It was then called "14-pound lake"; I caught more than a dozen of that size then!

The most effective pattern was fishing the giant topwater plugs in red head/white body and all yellow with red dot (called the clown) hues over a shallow shelf containing numerous laydowns. The waters ranged from 4 to 8 feet on the shelf and dropped off to 15 feet throughout the rest of the lake. A #18 Luhr-Jensen Pet Spoon fooled several of the big peacocks as well.

That afternoon, we moved to a land-locked lake named Lago Bacuri, where another comfortable aluminum flat-bottom boat awaited us. The 35 peacocks that we caught there averaged slightly smaller, 6 to 7 pounds, but a 12 1/2 and 13 pounder topped our tally. The topwater and spoon fare again produced, and a blue/silver Super Trap also fooled some of the larger peacocks. Most of the better fish were caught by either casting our lures to the middle of the lake or by trolling right down the center.

Over the final two days, we averaged around 35 peacock with half dozen or more weighing in at 12 pounds. We caught most of the big fish in Lago Comanda either trolling giant spoons, large jerkbaits and the Super Trap or by casting spoons and Big Game Woodchoppers to points

A temporary visitor to the lodge was the interesting three-toed sloth which hung around for almost a week before slowly crawling back into the nearby jungle.

with adjacent flats. Overall, my partner and I caught almost 300 peacock including over 40 above 10 pounds on that trip.

The Eyes Watching Us

Even with the fishing action, I am always amazed at the abundant wildlife on the Agua Boa. On my three trips to these waters, I have sited capybara scurrying along sandbars, several families of large otters playing in the lagoons and more than a few varieties of monkeys swinging through the surrounding trees. The forest creatures seemed to be intrigued by man in their territory.

There are reportedly 1,000 species of feathered, multicolored friends, and we saw many varieties including scarlet ibis, macaws, parrots and parakeets, huge black and white ducks, black and white herons, kingfishers, and other even more colorful birds not existing in the states. Many flapped away noisily from our presence. Several pairs of temporarily-departing macaws seemingly cursed at us as we motored along the twisting waterway by their roosts.

A sloth was temporarily relocated from a tree nearby to the Ecotur Park Lodge. It slowly climbed the support posts in search of leaves to nibble on. The friendly animal hung around the lodge for a few days

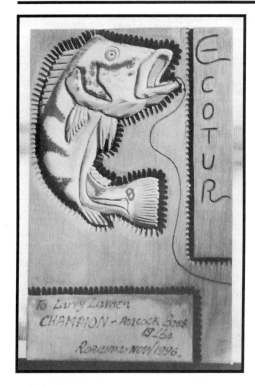

The lodge gives a unique plaque to all anglers which lists their largest peacock bass of the week. The one with the group's biggest is acclaimed "Champion".

before wandering back into the jungle. We chose not to look for other, more nocturnal sights such as jaguar, ocelot or anacondas.

Ecotur Park Lodge

The lodge is perched on a high riverside bluff beside a picturesque little spring run. It is just one of six very clear creeks entering the Agua Boa in the stretch adjacent to the state park.

Adjacent the lodge building are two perpendicular, private landing strips carved out of the Amazon rain forest for easy air access. The longest airfield can handle 20-passenger planes. Dr. Wilt is a pilot and, in fact, utilized a Corsario ultralight aircraft with pontoons to search out the area's best lakes and lagoons and to quickly check water levels away from camp.

The lodge will easily accommodate 8 anglers in four double rooms. A generator placed in the jungle away from the lodge handles the duties of electricity for the stoves, refrigerators, freezers, ice maker, fans, and lights. Each two rooms share a full bath. The kitchen is international as well as local, and fresh fruits, soft drinks, and bottled water are available in unlimited supply.

Shower water from the spring creek below is stored in a large water tank above the two-story facility. Fortunately for bathers, the showers have heating elements. Even in the jungle, the creek and river waters are not very warm. Large screened windows and electrical fans keep the rooms cool, and at night the normal temperature is in the lower seventies. A cool breeze is always blowing off the river, and a couple of nights during my stay were actually a bit chilly (by Florida standards).

Below And Above The Action

On my first trip to the area, I donned mask and snorkel and spent a couple of hours in one of the clear water lagoons near the lodge and in the spring-fed creek adjacent the park. In the 15-foot visibilities, I noticed large schools of piranha, the primitive-looking traira, disk-shape pacu, gold-scaled piraputanga, what appeared to be red-tail shiners and numerous other weird-looking fish species.

The waters of the lagoon and creek were teeming with small fish the size of the perfect 10- to 15-pound peacock bass forage. I also spotted a few peacock bass, a couple of freshwater stingrays and small catfish. I returned to Ecotur Park with a totally new sense of the underwater environment.

While those I spotted in the creek were small, many of the area's catfish get larger, very large. Jan's father, Rudy, may be the best catfisherman in northern Brazil. He often goes out in his boat and catches a variety of giant catfish such as pirarara, piraiba and pintado. In fact, while on my third trip to these waters, I too scored on pirarara or red-tail catfish. I caught a 20 and a 24 pounder on a minnow lure and a large Pet Spoon. Both fish put up strong, "bulldog" battles.

The waters of the river, creeks and lagoons are clearest during the dry season and the period of lowest water levels. That normally occurs on the Agua Boa from November through April, but "El Nino", "La Nina" and other factors can alter the weather and water levels. Also on that trip, I went up in a tiny ultralight aircraft with pontoons for a fascinating look at several of the lagoons and lakes near the lodge. We scooted about a few hundred yards up and had the proverbial "bird's eye" view of several "fishy" spots.

Dr. Wilt also books anglers into his operation on the Rio Tapara during the same months on one of his houseboats, and on a variety of other tributaries south of Manaus during the period from August to

December. Water is lowest is southern Brazil then and that region's peacock bass fishing is in its prime.

You need a valid passport and a visa to visit Brazil. To get additional details on the Ecotur Park Lodge on the Rio Agua Boa, contact Dick Ballard at Fishing Adventures, 140 E. Ritter, Republic, MO 65738 or phone (800) 336-9735.

In three visits to the Agua Boa, I have yet to fish more than about half of the area's 32 lagoons, resacas (oxbows) and land-locked lakes. When I can catch 30 to 50 peacock a day with many giants from just two or three, why look elsewhere. Fortunately, for the sake of conservation, Dr. Wilt has the guides rotate their pressure on the 32 lakes. Almost all are usually red hot!

Chapter 2

THE QUEEN'S RITES OF THE RAINFOREST

Jungle river boat antics on 20-pound monsters

The structure was classic: a 30-foot-long offshore bed of stickups on a hump positioned under 7 to 10 feet of water. I let the 1 3/4-ounce topwater plug sail toward the far point as my partner cast his to the near edge of the 1-inch-diameter trees. I twitched the Amazon Ripper once and the massive bass exploded on it, knocking the 7-inch tail-prop plug 4 feet into the air.

The plug landed about 8 feet closer to the boat, and I twitched it again quickly. To my dismay, my line had wrapped around the front treble.

I was about to twitch the plug anyway when the giant fish again smashed the bait. Instinctively, I set the hook and was solid to the monster peacock bass. The giant tore off toward the stickups, pulling 60-pound test line from my locked-down drag. Fortunately, the big fish turned and battled in open water for a minute before heading toward a deadfall on the bank behind our boat.

I didn't want to bully the fish too much given my seemingly precarious hookup, so I just kept steady pressure on him. The giant again turned away from the shoreside entanglements and wallowed on the surface. This time I saw that only one point of the treble hook held the fish. I feared the worst as the fish again powered toward the wooded hump. I turned the giant, and it shook the plug violently.

Fortunately, the hook held, and I worked the fish toward the net. The guide froze with net in hand when he saw the fish up close. The peacock shook its head twice and swam away from the net. With careful pressure, I turned the giant and brought it close to the waiting net. This time, my guide's aim was true, and the fish was lifted aboard.

T he 21-plus pounder that exploded on my big surface plug is one of three over 20 that I've taken on Amazon Queen trips.

My partner, Bill Wagner, grabbed our certified scales to weigh the fish (21 pounds) and measure it (36 inches long). We took a girth measurement (21 1/2 inches) and several photos before releasing the giant peacock. The fish from the Matupiri River south of Manaus in the middle of the Amazon rain forest was a new personal best for me. My previous top peacock was a 20-pounder, also 36 inches long.

A couple of days later on a nearby watershed, I caught another big peacock that measured 33 inches long and 21 inches in girth. That fish weighed 18 pounds and put up a similar escape effort. The big peacock jumped twice trying to cast off the 7-inch-long Big Game Woodchopper topwater plug.

I won that battle but was not so lucky a few other times during my week aboard the Amazon Queen, a luxury three-story jungle riverboat that carries up to 14 anglers to the world's most explosive freshwater fish. You win some and lose some when battling big peacock bass in the Brazilian Amazonia Region. That's the norm.

Big peacock bass roam the states of Para, Roraima and Amazonas in the South American country, and the action of a lifetime takes a toll on equipment and nerves. Battle stories ran rampant each night as the anglers sat on the Queen's upper deck refurbishing partially destroyed tackle and readying their arsenal for the next day's conflict.

One angler told of landing a 13-pounder on the front treble hook of his Big Game Woodchopper and a 3-pounder on its tail hook. The smaller fish struck the bait first, and the big one tried to snatch it away. Tales of guides going overboard to retrieve big fish from submerged brush were common. One dove twice into an entanglement in 8 feet of water to bring up a 16-pounder. Another went swimming for his client's 15-pounder and again for a 16-pounder hung up in a submerged tree.

Hooks were ripped from the most stout of plugs, split rings torn open, lines testing less than about 60 pounds were snapped, hooks were straightened and rods broken. The fish were victorious in most of the battles, but several trophies were captured, photographed and released.

Big Fish Tally

In all, our 14 anglers fishing the rivers of Amazonas south of Manaus caught 72 peacock bass over 10 pounds, including 26 in the 15- to 19-pound category. Seven weighed better than 20 pounds. Our group landed and released 539 fish in the five-day trip. Ward Lang of Duluth, Georgia, took the largest of the trip, a 24-pounder that was just 3 pounds off the world record. He was fishing a Big Game Woodchopper near a large emergent tree when the giant exploded on the 7-inch plug.

Larry Easter and partner David Taylor, both of Dallas, Texas, happened on a large school of giant peacock bass on their first day on the Rio Prato. They caught peacocks weighing 13, 14, 15, 16, 20 and 21 pounds from a long, flooded strip of big offshore trees. The 200-yard submerged island varied from about 2 to 10 feet deep and yielded big fish all along its skinny perimeter. Easter garnered the two largest that day, but the most exciting strike was one of Taylor's 16-pounders that jumped 4 feet into the air and landed, mouth open, on the big Woodchopper plug. The two returned the following day to catch and release four more in the 15- to 16-pound category.

"All of the 33 fish over 15 pounds caught this week in the rivers south of Manaus were taken on giant Luhr-Jensen topwater plugs," said Amazon Queen owner/operator Phil Marsteller. "The Big Game Woodchopper accounted for 25 of the big fish, and the Amazon Ripper the remainder. The preferred lure color was yellow with dots, called by the manufacturer, the "clown" pattern. The fire tiger and the black with orange belly hues were close behind in productivity."

The often mirror-smooth lagoons are usually very productive. Fishing the edges of a wall of trees with laydowns and overhanging limbs often yields my biggest fish of the week. There are plenty of such spots off the Rio Negro and Marsteller's guides know where they are.

The Rio Negro area of Brazil offers the most exciting peacock bass fishing in the world. Topwater hungry giants that live in the black-clear waters of the Amazon tributaries can make any trip exciting and memorable. Bass anglers can get spoiled easily in the jungle. But keep in mind that it is jungle!

On several occasions, my native guide has steered the fiberglass bass boat into a wooded pocket that seemingly ended abruptly. There, he quickly moves to the bow and employs a machete to clear a narrow passageway for our egress into a hidden lagoon. He chops vines and limbs in the brushy tunnel while I and my partner pull and push the boat forward in the canopied darkness. We emerge over an entanglement of fallen limbs into the forest-surrounded water hole.

End of Season Battle

On my most recent trip aboard the Amazon Queen in March of 1998, water was very low due to El Nino and we did have to cut our way into a couple of lagoons. In others, we didn't have enough water to access them. I did catch some giant peacocks, so the trip was very memorable.

In one small lagoon, called "Lago Mon", my Woodchopper was catapulted straight up as the water on which it had laid erupted. Two greenish yellow torpedoes hell-bent on destroying the "intruder" knocked the 7-inch lure skyward. It was in the middle of a one-and-one-half gainer some two feet above the tannin-stained water when another giant peacock exploded through the surface and struck its target squarely.

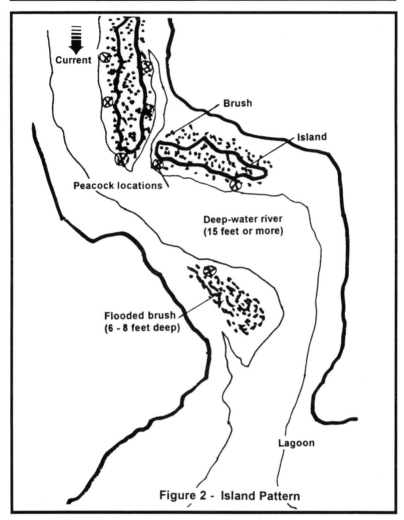

Figure 2 - Island Pattern

Figure 2 - The Madeira watershed is composed of numerous rivers with oxbow channels, islands and submerged brush. The better peacock bass areas offer a quick drop to deep water, islands, points and flooded brush. The largest peacocks are usually just inside the brush out of any current. Cast a giant topwater lure upstream to the shallows and bring it into the pockets or areas of sparse brush. This pattern has proven itself time and again in these waters and others in South America.

A strict catch and release policy is vital to the longevity of any giant peacock bass fishery. Anglers aboard the Amazon Queen catch more than their share of monster fish and their guides are well trained in conservation of the species.

I instantly struck back to plant the large 4\0 trebles in the jaws that appeared big enough to swallow the watermelon that our group had snacked on at the previous night's dinner.

I battled the 18 pound, 31 1/2 inch long (21 1/2 inch girth) peacock through two brush piles to the boat. Off another brushy shoreline in Lago Keyounee, I caught my largest fish of that week. The 20 pounder, taken on a red-and-white Big Game Woodchopper measured 33 inches in length and 23 inches in girth.

Another 18 pounder was taken from a huge laydown in Lago Monquarui. I was casting a peacock-design Woodchopper to which I had added some orange deer hair on the tail treble. I helped Luhr-Jensen come up with the "peacock" color scheme, but then, that's another story. I twitched the bait twice when the monster hit and went straight for the trunk's underbelly. I won that battle, weighed and measured the fish (33 inches long and 21 inch girth) before releasing it.

Other catches of our 14-person group that week included two 18's, a 19, a 20 and a 22 pounder on perch-colored Big Game Woodchoppers, and 17, 19 and 20 pound peacocks on black back/orange belly Rippers. There was also an 18 pounder caught on a 6 1/2 inch Redfin minnow bait.

Low Water Tactics

Most of our catch came from the Rio Negro's sandbar islands with deep water adjacent, from points and bars, and from huge laydowns in the low-level waters. Some sand bars were shaped by the current to have gear teeth appearance. Fishing such is a great low-water pattern if there is sufficient depth behind the sand bars.

Since the waters at the tail-end of the season were extremely shallow, lures that are typically very productive at normal levels were less than effective. Rat-L-Traps were not successful, nor were any lures being trolled behind the 17-foot Nitro boats. The water was just too low. Actions was spotty, but some spots were active.

On one spot, I hooked a peacock on my big topwater plug, handed the rod to my guide as the fish neared the boat, and then used a Redfin minnow "comeback" lure for the second peacock of my one-person, two-cast double. The two fish weighed about 14 pounds total. I went on to catch and release five peacock from that spot. That's not two fish on one plug, but the timing is close.

The largest legitimate "double" on a single plug that I have heard of were two fish weighing 16 and 19 pounds that hit a Big Game Woodchopper on an earlier Amazon Queen trip. On another occasion, according to Marsteller, a Queen angler caught a 15 and 18 pounder on the same plug on one cast. Still another angler caught a 12 pound and 8 pound speckled peacock on the front two trebles and a 2 pound butterfly on the Woodchopper's rear treble hook. I guess when the water is low, the fish get hungry.

"Our dry season started a little early, so the low water levels that we should have reached in April came in January," explains Marsteller. "Normally in December, the water level rises about five or six feet and then drops back down, which is what we call 'voiacu'. In 1998, we finally had our season's first voiacu in February."

"The low water after the first of the year affected the numbers of peacock," he admits, "because we couldn't access the lagoons that we normally fish. We had to stay in the main river channels where there are fewer fish. The peacocks mostly stay back in the lagoons which have deep areas in them. The smaller ones and even some of the bigger fish couldn't get out and we couldn't get in to them."

Monsters, like the author's 20 pound Rio Negro peacock, are normally taken on topwater plugs, such as the popular Big Game Woodchopper.

"So, your total week's quantity was cut in half due to the low water," he told me. "During the extremely low water in January, February and March, we still averaged about six to seven fish a week over 20 pounds. Our total fish count average dropped to about 650 fish a week, whereas we were averaging about 14 fish over 20 and right around a thousand fish a week in October through December."

Amazing Giant Fish Production

Despite the low water, the Amazon Queen had its best year ever during their most recent "season" that stretched 22 weeks from October 1997 to April 1998. Anglers aboard the Queen accounted for a total of 19,112 peacock caught and mostly released which included 5 that reportedly weighed 25 or 26 pounds and another 23 that topped 23 pounds.

The Queen's anglers caught 113 fish weighing 20 pounds, 53 weighing 21 pounds and 27 that hit the 22 pound mark. Those are truly monster fish, considering that the world record is 27 pounds, but the 732 peacocks between 15 and 20 pounds that Queen anglers caught are worthy giants as well.

In the 1996/1997 season, anglers aboard the Amazon Queen averaged "only" three peacocks over 20 pounds each week, even with higher water. During the 1997/1998 season, the Queen's anglers averaged about 10 fish over 20 pounds per week for the season even with the low water in January through March which substantially reduced the numbers of big fish.

"We have never before had a season with this type of incredible fishing," notes Marsteller. "On our best week's trip, we landed 29 peacock over 20 pounds each. Our largest fish of the season weighed 26.9 pounds!"

Spawning Times

The giant peacocks fortunately don't lose weight after spawning; the giants are males. Like largemouth and other species, peacock bass are difficult to catch while on the beds not feeding, but not after the spawning process. In one area off the Rio Negro where the water level had dropped, I noticed five small beds within a huge bed on an exposed sand bar. The guide noted that the butterfly peacocks had been using the larger acu peacock bed to save clearing time. The bed of five of the smaller specie fit easily into the large one.

Fortunately, peacocks don't all bed at the same time, so crowds on the spawning grounds can be minimal. The butterfly peacocks tend to spawn closer together in location and in time over just a couple of weeks. The giant speckled or "paca" and grande or "acu" peacocks usually spawn within a month of each other, but just when they go on their beds and spawn is not based on a specific time.

It's based on the water level from September through April and upon when it starts dropping, according to Marsteller. Any time the water drops substantially, more than 3 or 4 feet, a spawn usually occurs one month later. In 1997 and 1998, for example, there were several spawns along a fluctuating Rio Negro and evidence of spawn lasted most of the season.

That post-spawn evidence may be old beds, or it may be the parents swimming around with their fry on the surface. An angler can detect the fry making tiny ripples or dimples in the lagoon's surface. And, unless one of them has already been caught and kept, there will be a male and female with the small peacocks.

Sight Fishing Post-Spawners

Sight fishing for these giant post-spawn fish can be challenging, exciting and productive. Casting to tiny ripples or "bubbles" breaking the dark surface can result in some great action. The small surface ripples are made by the cruising fry. When the school is disturbed, the parent will gather up the fry or fingerlings in their mouths and move away from the commotion. However, if the lure hits down close enough to appear dangerous to the newborn, the furious parent will explode on the lure.

Then, the battle may rage in open water, and the angler has a chance to land the often giant peacock. Be prepared for a fight though, as I found out when a 20 plus pounder broke my heavy line after the hook-up.

If you are fishing a topwater plug, cast it about 3 feet beyond the tiny ripples and make long, "ripping" sweeps of the rod (rather than short jerks). A mad parent will try to destroy the plug instantaneously, or you will not get a response. I caught two this way on my last trip to the Rio Negro and then released them so they could return to their "bambinos."

If you are tossing a big minnow bait, try to place it right on top of the bubbles and then quickly jerk it one time. You will get the strike then, or else you will not get the strike. Once you land the post-spawn fish, quickly release it. The fry and the other parent are waiting.

The Rio Negro Lodge

The Rio Negro Lodge lies about 60 miles west north west of Barcelos on the southern bank of the Rio Negro. It has eight air conditioned guest cabins and one central lodge, dining and bar area. The 900 square foot cabins are spread along the bank, with 150 feet between each. They each have a large main living area and a large bathroom.

Inside are two queen beds, a small bar area, card table area, couch and loveseat. The bathroom has a two-person jacuzzi-type tub, double sinks, commode area, shower stall and large walk-in closet. All have open beamed ceilings and big glass windows that look out over the Rio Negro. The trees are thinned for guests to enjoy a view of the river, but dense enough for privacy from the passing boats.

"This lodge is geared more toward privacy and toward couples," says Marsteller. "We'll accommodate two persons per cabin. The main lodge area of over 4,000 square feet has the kitchen, an office, a tackle area, a gift shop area, a bar and the dining area. We have all exposed beamed ceilings, air conditioning, big glass windows looking out over a grassed area, and a large swimming pool."

"The dock area is going to be a floating dock that will beattached to the stone steps going up the side of the bank," he continues. "It will be set up for the Amazon Queen to tie up and will have individual boat slips for each of our Nitro bass boats. The new lodge also has a private 4,500 foot runway within a mile."

"I'm sure that a peacock bass operation will work here long term," Marsteller confides. "That's why we based the Queen in this area for most of the '97/'98 season. We fished all season long except for the first week strictly from the lodge location to make sure it could handle the fishing pressure. We have a huge area to fish."

T hree-bar peacocks make huge beds that may be high and dry when water levels drop. Fortunately, peacock bass are not on beds long.

Some of the better areas you can easily reach from the lodge include the Rio Cuiuni, which lies south of the Rio Negro, a tributary to the North called the Rio Araca and its tributary, the Rio Itu, and the Rio Ariraha to the west. The Erere and Padauari Rivers are right at the lodge's back door, and there are hundreds of lagoons off those tributaries and the main Rio Negro. An hour away to the southeast is the Rio Dimini which also has lots of additional tributaries and lagoons.

"We haven't fished 10 percent of the lagoons and lakes in this area yet," notes Marsteller. "The lodge is smack in the heart of our prime northern fishery, so the Queen will probably fish one or two days a week fairly close to where the lodge is. But, the Queen will run a lot more, farther east and farther west."

Much more on the Rio Negro and the Amazon Queen appears in chapters 1 and 6 of my book, "Peacock Bass & Other Fierce Exotics". For more information on the Amazon Queen or the Rio Negro Lodge, contact Amazon Tours at P.O. Box 3106, Coppell, TX 75019; (972) 304-1656.

Chapter 3

ACROBATICS ON THE RIO SAO BENEDITO

Put your shades on for this non-stop excitement

Two crimson-red depth charges raced from beneath the floating vegetation, exploding on my surface plug. I blinked as my eyeballs focused on the washtub-size hole that replaced the 5 1/2 inch Amazon Ripper. A taut braid frantically cut the water away from the spot as a single, very upset fish made its anger clear to me.

Taking to the air in several frantic attempts to relieve itself of the big lure, the vividly-hued peacock destroyed the ambiance of the quiet little lagoon. Disturbed water birds on the lagoon's vegetated perimeter took flight and voiced their disdain for the interruption by fish and angler. The commotion continued as the peacock pulled drag in the depths, pausing only go airborne time and time again.

Tiring from six or seven explosive jumps and the steady pressure of my seemingly futile efforts to gain control of the battle, the peacock finally neared the boat. The fish made one last dive toward the depths before my guide secured it with a long-nose, plier-like grabber. The brilliantly-colored Fogo (or fire) peacock bass was my first of that particular species and it was a big one. It weighed 9 1/4 pounds on my certified scales just prior to release.

Nowhere else will you find the Fogo peacock other than in the Sao Benedito watershed, which is an Amazon tributary in the states of Para and Mato Grosso in southern Brazil. The fish grows only to 10 or 11 pounds.

The fire peacock are a beautiful specimen "painted" with dramatic crimson red on their belly, jaw and lower fins and gold with black specks on their upper side and back. The fish, also called "tucunare vermilho" in Brazil, is different from the commonly caught peacocks of the Amazon

T he fogo or "fire" peacock bass is an exciting species that has the markings of a both a butterfly and speckled peacock but only grows to 10 or 11 pounds. The author's first one was a 9-1/4 pounder.

and Florida. While some fire peacock have the three large rosettes similar to the butterfly peacock, they also have the black gill cover splotches of a speckled peacock. Their bodies are different from both. A fire peacock has a chunkier body than either.

My quest to capture one of the fire peacocks for which the Sao Benedito is famous actually took two trips. The 9 1/4 pounder came within five minutes of my first day's fishing on the second trip in August. My first trip to explore the unspoiled waters took place in late March, the perfect time to experience a variety of other big freshwater gamefish swimming in higher water conditions.

On that first trip, giant payara, or "Dracula" fish, and huge bicuda shot skyward like rockets when hooked in the river bends. The aerial show was part of an exciting week that included daily catches of six or seven species. The menacing-looking payara, or "cachorra" as it is called in Brazil, averaged 7 to 9 pounds in most areas of the Sao Benedito and its tributary the Rio Azul or Blue River. But on my first trip, my partner booking agent Dick Ballard and I caught several larger payara in the mid to upper teens. From January through May, the larger ones are concentrated in the river.

The high-jumping bicuda, a slender fish with a pointed, "beak-like" snout, averaged six pounds or so, but my largest of the week appeared to be around 12 pounds. It threw a 6 1/2 inch long Redfin after a series of strong runs and spectacular leaps. Ballard and I caught most of our bicuda in deep, backwater holes adjacent to the deep pools below areas of rocks and rapids. The fish seem to prefer an "upstream" current caused by an eddy. They are extremely difficult to keep on and land.

On my second trip, while fishing with Wylie Phillips, an oil company executive currently living in Bogota, Colombia, the river waters were lower and the payara and bicuda slightly smaller. Our top payara-catcher during the week were Redfins and the hotspots were deep, deadfall-laden curves in the Blue River. The slashers put pin holes in several of our minnow baits and were extremely wild when hooked, leaping throughout the turbulence of the heavy current in the river's outer bends.

Our casts to the downstream, current-blocked side of the fallen trees were most productive on payara of around 8 pounds and bicuda averaging around 5 pounds. In rapids or rocks, both of these aggressive fish are equally explosive.

World Record Fish

During low water and mid-height water levels, Sao Benedito's currents yield other great sport fish such as the corvina. The fish, whose common name is "silver croaker" looks like a freshwater drum and averages around 6 pounds. Fishing just above the rapids that lie 1/2 mile upstream of our lodge, the Pousada Salto Thaimacu, I was lucky enough to capture a new All-Tackle IGFA world record for the species. The strong fighter, caught on a giant Super Trap, weighed 9 pounds and measured 28 inches.

This area of the Amazon Basin produces a greater variety of large gamefish species than any other in the world! The waters of the Sao Benedito and Blue rivers vary in depth from 3 to 25 feet and greatly in current speed and bottom structure. While the payara grow to around 30 pounds, catfish grow much larger.

"We've caught suribim up to 39 pounds, pirarara up to 44 pounds and pintado up to around 34 pounds," says lodge owner-operator Carlos Munhos Arroyo. "Piraiba catfish grow to almost 50 pounds and the Jau can reach 55 pounds in these waters. Some catfish will actively feed during daylight hours and have been known to strike lures, but the best fishing is at night on cut bait."

Typically, though, the catfish here average 12 to 25 pounds, and the best times are July through September for suribim and January through April for the others. In my two trips, I caught 3 different catfish species that topped out at around 12 pounds. During my week in August, two pintado of 20 to 22 pounds were taken during the day by Brazilian catfishermen.

The author caught this All-Tackle IGFA world record corvina or silver croaker. The strong fighter, caught on a giant Super Trap, weighed 9 pounds and measured 28 inches.

In these waters, there are also traira or "trairao", as they are known in Brazil. Like peacock bass, they prefer slow or no current. The ugly, prehistoric-looking fish average around 8 pounds but reportedly grow to a maximum of 37 1/2 pounds in the Rio Sao Benedito. I caught two 12 pounders in one lagoon, and Wylie caught a 14 pounder from the same area. Like the peacock, payara and bicuda, the traira will tear up all types of lures and go wild when hooked. It will jump frequently with the aid of its giant tail and put on a show you won't forget.

Another big battle waiting to happen is the formidable pacu, which resembles a huge piranha and weighs as much as 10 or 11 pounds. The piranha average 2 to 3 pounds but "max" out at almost 9 pounds, adding to the excitement of the watershed. Both are commonly caught with diving or sinking lures in moving waters. Tambaqui averaging 8 pounds each and sometimes pushing the low teens may liven up the fishing experience, as well.

During my first trip when waters were too high for finding peacocks in the lagoons, Ballard, Pete Herber of Des Moines Iowa, and I focused for a couple of days on a Brazilian favorite which actively feed in schools. From January though April, the feisty matrinxa average 3 to 5 pounds, but a few grow to over 10. We all caught several each day on spinners and spoons fished on light tackle. The popular sportfish is a lot to handle on light tackle.

Another light tackle sportfish is the jacunda, and I was lucky enough to catch two species of them. Several fish of about one pound were the colorful version with yellows, greens and golds, and one specimen was a silver hue with one giant black spot near its tail. Two of our jacunda were half eaten by piranha by the time we got them to the boat!

Dick Ballard tussled with numerous feisty matrinxa in the Sao Benedito River. Small spoons were the attractant to the fish which averages 4 pounds or so.

Firecracker Dispositions

The fire peacock, though, are the real "firecrackers." Like most species of peacock, they are caught on topwater lures during low-water periods in and around the numerous blackwater lagoons and lakes. They are found in the lagoons, and along the river in quiet spots, inner bends with pockets and points of vegetation.

In August, they were my focus. My tally for the 5 1/2 days included 45 peacock bass including the 9 1/4 and an 8 1/4 pounder, 20 payara, the IGFA world record silver croaker, and 24 other specimens of four different species. Ninety percent of the peacocks were the beautiful "fire" version.

Wylie took around 20 peacocks, and almost as many payara and piranha, as well as an 8 pound corvina (silver croaker). The other Americans in the camp were avid anglers Earl and Dot Bean. They caught about 60 peacocks and several other species of fish from the Sao Benedito.

The fire peacocks were mostly found in the lagoons, specifically in the mouths of the small lakes, and along the river in quiet spots, inner bends with pockets and points of vegetation, and shallow sloughs at the edge of the current. Top water plugs, like the Ripper and the Jerkin' Sam, along with Rat-L-Traps and a small spinnerbait worked well on the fish.

*N*owhere else will you find the brilliantly-colored fogo (or fire) peacock other than in the Amazon's Sao Benedito watershed in southern Brazil. Their markings are unique.

In general, smaller lures than those used in other Amazon regions seemed to work best.

We caught a few of the Amazon's more common peacocks, the butterfly and the speckled (called "paca" tucunare). While the average peacock bass in the lagoons and river weighs between 3 and 6 pounds, the largest reportedly taken by a lodge guest was a giant 13 1/2 pounder.

Both the Blue and Sao Benedito rivers are small waterways where noisy green parrots race by above the archway of trees that frequently crowd the twisting waterways. Pairs of scarlet macaws, among the largest of South American parrots at three-feet long, move from nearby treetops and wheel overhead making all the racket they can muster as you drift through river pools. Occasionally, blue and yellow macaws, canary-winged parakeets and colorful toucans brightened the skies, while several beautiful electric-blue morpho butterflies skirted the river's edge and fluttered around us.

The Rio Sao Benedito, which averages 5 foot in depth, is a tributary of the Teles Pires River, a large tributary of the huge Tapajos River in the State of Para, Brazil's second largest. The Sao Benedito is an exciting fishery with its clear-water rivers encompassing a number of waterfalls, sandy, rocky-bottomed streams, spring-fed lagoons and creeks, deep pools and grass-lined lakes.

Salto Thaimacu Isolation

Pousada Salto Thaimacu Lodge is located on a privately-owned ranch of 25,000 acres right on the river in front of Thaimacu Falls. A short distance away from the three-year old facility lies Salto do Pista Falls. The remote fishing camp lodge is an extremely isolated "oasis", which corresponds to very little fishing pressure and lots of fishing action!

Just 40 miles downstream from the lodge is the Caiabi Indian village near the river's juncture with the Teles Pires. Located in the "blue-water" region of the southeast Amazonas, the headwaters of the Sao Benedito are in the Brazilian highlands. There are 7 medium-size lagoons averaging 15 feet in depth that connect via short creeks to the Sao Benedito.

The river and its tributaries Rio Azul (Blue River) and Rio Cururu-Acu (Big Frog River) are beautiful rivers that are loaded with aggressive fish. Sandbars and fallen timber in the bends, slow the currents in places on the Blue River, and the upper stretches are more reminiscent of trout streams with clear waters flowing over long, rocky rapids. It is here, about 3 1/2 hours from camp, where you can see most every strike and watch it from the initial follow. Strikes occur from a variety of species on almost every cast.

The Blue River, and the lagoons off of it, offers a tremendous quantity and variety of fish, amidst a colorful enviro-scape of birds and wildlife.

The prime season for sportfishing this region south of the Equator is during their low-water months (June through October). Topwater action is excellent for most species of gamefish during their winter and spring times. While peacock bass and traira usually prefer slow-moving and low water lagoon habitat, all other sportfish of the region can be caught as early as April and May and as late as November.

Accessing The Excitement

From the air, you will see the beautiful clear rivers winding through deep valleys of the rain forest. You will see forested hills, waterfalls and

Payara, or "cachorra" as they are called in Brazil, may reach 20 pounds in the Sao Benedito River. A pretty angler caught this menacing-looking one.

rapids and miles and miles of lush, green-canopied rainforest. Only guests of the lodge can access this region of the Amazon.

Reaching the remote lodge via a short, 25-minute charter flight from Alta Floresta in the state of Mato Grosso is a no-hassle experience. The camp landing strip was bulldozed out of the jungle by Arroyo. Alta Floresta, a community of 60,000 people offers daily commercial air service to/from Belem, Brazil and Sao Paulo, and daily commercial flights between those gateways and Miami make the isolated lodge convenient to U.S. sportfishermen.

About the only thing to interfere with the flights are possible burnings in the areas around the city. "Queimadas" are harmful prescribed burnings that are based on a primitive method of preparing the soil for the next season's crops. This takes place over a few weeks in our summer.

Pousada Salto Thaimacu offers excellent service, facilities and management. Arroyo, a cattle farmer, has built a very comfortable Pousada Salto Thaimacu Lodge which offers four, two-bedroom cabins with private bath and a lodge house with 4 guest rooms, in all housing up to 20 guests.

The modern lodge has a separate kitchen and main dining room and a delicious "Americanized" menu. Three meals are served daily and full laundry service is available. Three 40 kva lodge generators provide power to the guest quarters for air conditioning, lights, hot water showers, and to the lodge kitchen/dining room for the ice makers, refrigerators, freezers, etc.

At the lodge marina are 14 roomy and carefully laid out 16-foot aluminum bass boats. They all come ready to fish with 25-hp motors, electric trolling motors, comfortable swivel seats and very knowledgeable guides. Your tackle should be sturdy and up to the task of handling the fish which will range from 3 to over 20 pounds. Bring plenty of line and steel leaders for the toothy critters that will try to carry your tackle away.

The guide controls the boat and the cooler stocked fully with ice, refreshments and lunch. Those fishing close to camp can return to the lodge dining room for the noon meal. Should you want to go after some real monsters, try fishing in the evening for giant catfish. Very stout tackle is required for such a venture.

A bilingual translator is with you at the camp and in Alta Floresta. Fishing guides do not speak English, but translation information sheets are provided in each boat.

In Harmony With Nature

Conservation of the fabulous sport fishery in the waterways of this virgin rainforest is extremely important to the operator. As a result, Brazilian sportfishermen and U.S. fishermen are required to practice catch and release fishing on these waters. The exception may be a few fish kept for an evening meal and some of the "non-sportfish" species, such as catfish.

What you will not see along the shores of the Sao Benedito are native residents. What you will see around the water in the uninhabited region are "jacare'" (caiman), fresh water rays, turtles, snakes, eels, frogs and otters. At the water's edge, tapirs and capybaras scramble into the jungle and butterflies flit about, and in the trees, you may spy a small band of one of the several species of monkeys and/or iguanas and sloths.

After the sun sets, you can sometimes hear the sounds of jaguars, ocelots and panthers roaming the jungle floor. Tarantulas, beetles and moths move about the nearby trees. A couple of anglers in our party saw a black panther during daylight. In daylight, javelins, anteaters, and deer stroll through the forest. The bird life commonly seen in the watershed includes macaws, toucans, parrots, herons, hummingbirds, ibis (pink and white), kingfishers, jaburi storks, soldier storks, vultures, eagles, hawks, parakeets, and ducks.

The hoatzins which resemble a kind of turkey with skinny neck and head comb are seemingly everywhere along the waterways. In masses of up to 50 birds, they rustle overhead from one waterfront tree to another along the lagoons and river.

Arroyo and his son are excellent fishermen and sportsmen, and they too can help you get ready for the fishing adventure. For information on this adventure, contact Dick Ballard at Fishing Adventures, 140 E. Ritter, Republic, MO 65738 or phone (800) 336-9735.

Imagine what an Amazon tributary that is uninhabited and unspoiled by man, should be like. Pousada Salto Thaimacu offers one of the few examples of the untamed, unspoiled Amazon dream that still exists today. There is little evidence of the encroachment of man, so this oasis remains a preserved stronghold of the wild and unconquered Amazon.

Chapter 4

CLIPPIN' ALONG WITH RAW POWER

Long charges, big jaws and pockets of peacocks in the Rio Uatuma

A huge boil swept my lure one foot to the side. I kept twitching the seven inch long topwater in a cadence that I felt sure would draw another strike. This giant of a bass was my quarry for the week in the Brazilian rainforest. It was my last day on the Rio Uatuma and time was quickly running out.

A peacock bass weighing in the teens is a prize I always cherish on my trips to the Amazon Basin, and I knew such a fish now existed within my cast's reach. I moved the lure another ten feet before a smaller stout peacock exploded on the bait, beating the larger fish to it. One second later, a huge fish exploded on my partner's surface lure which was being twitched similarly just 10 feet away.

"Double," we shouted simultaneously. "Both are big fish."

We battled our peacocks to the boat and our guide, Harold, slipped the net first under C. Wayne Nolan's fish and then mine. As he struggled to lift the pair in the net, it broke from the combined 24-pound weight. The two fish weighed 13 1/2 and 10 1/2 pounds respectively, which is not a bad "double".

After about 5 minutes of photo-taking and 10 minutes of big fish revival, it was time to make another cast into the area that consisted of a sandy bank with a breeze blowing a surface chop parallel with it. I lofted my Woodchopper back into the "double" spot and jerked it twice. The shower of spray from the lure's tailspinner hadn't fallen back to the surface when an even bigger explosion occurred in a flash of gold.

C. Wayne Nolan took his largest peacock, a 13 1/2 pounder, from a feeding flat off the Rio Uatuma, a tributary of the mighty Amazon.

I set the hook as my heretofore "quiet" drag whined and my 60-pound test UltraMax peeled from my casting reel. The first test of my new M5600C Morrum's drag was successful as the monster headed down the bank, jumping three times and then charging into what appeared to be obstruction-free depths. None of my 18 peacocks between 9 and 12 pounds taken earlier in the week had come close to pulling the tightened-down drag. I knew this was a giant bass.

Praying for a bottom without any ragged rocks, I kept pressure on the fish that seemed to be unaffected by this angler. I had lost another giant earlier that morning when I cast to a rocky point, and after exploding on the plug, the fish bore into a field of huge jagged rocks. The line stretched to its limit and the rock's razor sharp edges cut through it instantaneously. I didn't want to see a replay on what was my second chance of the week to catch a giant.

This monster peacock went where it wanted for about five minutes and at one point had 50 yards of my braid. Finally, after two more impressive leaps, the fish tired and succumbed to my pressure. Our guide slipped the net under the trophy and we all shouted in glee.

The giant male peacock bass had the big spawning knot on its forehead and a broad girth of 22 inches. We taped the length at 34 inches, and it weighed 19 1/4 pounds on our certified scales. After some quick photos, the fish was released to swim back to its lair. My trophy, which was my last fish of the last day of the week, easily eclipsed a 15 1/2 pounder as the trip's biggest bass by our 14-angler group.

Nolan, an avid bass tournament fisherman from Lewisville, Texas, was the group's leader and my partner for the week. While it was his first trip to Brazil, he caught on to the ways of the peacock bass quickly. We caught and released a total of around 70 peacocks and landed 24 that weighed over 9 pounds each.

The guides reported that our group that week caught 408 peacocks, of which 53 were 10 pounds or better. Some of the other top catches included the 15 1/2 pounder by Randy Stutts on our second afternoon, a 15 pounder by Brian Kowalski on the third day, and a 13 1/2 pounder by John Moore, all of Nashville, TN. Tom Kotlarsz, of Winston Salem, N.C., caught a 14 1/2 pound peacock on the fourth day, and several others caught 13 pounders, which were their personal best.

Surface Bite

All of the "teeners" were caught on big Luhr-Jensen Big Game Woodchoppers with single tail-spinners. The productive lure colors varied and included firetiger, blue and silver, black and orange, and red and white. Generally, it's the action that attracts the peacock bass.

On day three, Nolan and I found a concentration of big peacock on a wind-blown point in a large lagoon we called "Cattle Fence Lake" off the upper Uatuma River. We caught and released 12 bass averaging around 9 pounds each and had numerous other blow-ups, but one bit of action easily stands out in my mind.

I had cast toward the point and had started my surface retrieve in the three foot deep water when a big fish boiled on the Woodchopper but missed. Keeping my cool, I continued its movement in the same cadence and again garnered the strike. I was expecting the explosion, saw the lure disappear in the boil and set the hook, mostly out of instinct.

The lure came flying back at me, and I felt bad. The correct response should have been to set the hook only upon feeling the fish, because when the lure is jerked more than 10 feet away from the strike, the peacock can't follow it further.

"I blew it," I admitted to Nolan, as the plug splashed down three foot from the bow of the boat and I attempted to quickly reel in the slack line. "I just jerked it away from.."

An instantaneous explosion on the lure that had sailed over 30 feet in the air interrupted my statement of remorse. Five more seconds of frantic reeling put about 15 feet of tight line between me and the "hot" 10 pound peacock. It was a wild battle at boatside that I won; the fantastic fish had traveled further and faster after its quarry than any other I have ever seen. I pity any forage moving in front of that predator.

Action during the week was sporadic. The first two days were slow, but Nolan and I found a few concentrations of peacock on the other days. Points with either large emergent timber or a wind-born chop were productive as were those with large rocks and ragged boulders.

We had cast repeatedly on one point without success when our trolling motor hit a rock outcropping 50 feet from the nearest observable boulder. The guide shut off the motor as I took my rod with lure reeled to the tip and pointed it downward to determine the depth we were in. The tip and lure hit the bottom off the bow about four feet down, plenty of water to again employ our trolling motor.

Then, as I unsuspectingly lifted my rod tip to the surface, a five pound peacock grabbed the submerged Woodchopper. I reflexively flinched and jerked the startled fish into the air which released its grip on my topwater lure and swam back into the depths. That's the first time I've ever "vertical-fished" a floating topwater bait beside the boat with success!

Unusual things happen in the Amazon Region of Brazil. Our group of anglers were staying aboard the "Amazon Clipper" houseboat and fishing lagoons and river areas of the Uatuma each morning and afternoon from seven 17-foot Aluma-Weld bass boats powered by 55 and 60 horsepower outboards.

Unique Sightings

The Uatuma and its tributaries are an interesting watershed. Each day, white and yellow butterflies flit about as the sun rises and mud banks are exposed from a dropping water level. Kingfishers fly from tree to tree down the river's overgrown shoreline as our boat motors toward the fishing grounds. Herons occasionally take to the air and large black and white ducks in groups of three to six are sometimes spooked from their favorite paddling areas. A pair of macaws may fly by or a flock of parakeets or green parrots may skirt along overhead.

At dusk, fish-eating bats skim the river, and upon darkness settling in, the secretive creatures in the trees and along the bank venture out from their hiding places. In fact, much of the wildlife in the rainforest jungle are nocturnal. Big cats such as the ocelot or jaguar are fairly rare (I've only seen their tracks), but tapir and capybara are sometimes sighted in low light and after dark.

Tiny brilliantly-colored tropical fish feed on bugs in the shallows at night and are seen primarily by those using a flashlight. Some bigger fish that have obtained size by being cautious may be startled and dart off or even jump from the water when hit with the beam of a powerful

The author's big 19 1/4 pound peacock bass was seduced by a 2-ounce Woodchopper with yellow "clown" color pattern. No other lure is responsible for more giant peacock in any watershed.

flashlight. In fact, a two-foot long silvery fish spooked from Nolan's spotlight one night, leaped from the surface and hit him in the side of the head. He was in the bow of one of the fishing boats and moving closer to a little caiman for better observation of the reptile.

"I thought its momma had come and got me," relates the 55-year old Texan. "The baby gator was only two feet long and I could only see her in the spotlight as I leaned over to take a better look. Then, out of the darkness comes this explosion in my face. The other four wildlife observers aboard couldn't stop laughing."

Fortunately, the jumping fish was not the toothy kind and Nolan soon regained his composure after the experience. Most fish in the Amazon environment have either offensive weapons such as needle-sharp teeth, poison, pointed spines, or they possess superior maneuverability and/or speed. In the rainforest jungle waterways, the tough species survived and the weak died out thousands of years ago.

A common sight on the Uatuma during daylight hours are pink dolphin or "boto" (pronounced "bow too") that roll lazily in the main river and lagoon channels. The powerful and intelligent freshwater

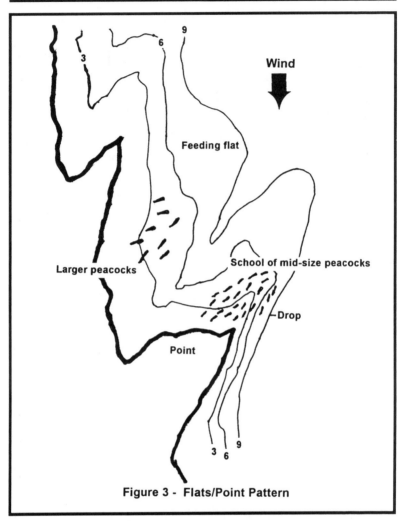

Figure 3 - Flats/Point Pattern

Figure 3 - The flats and points of the Uatuma and its tributaries are prime peacock spots when fishing pressure is minimal and water levels right. Deep water is usually near the sandy points. Mid-size peacocks concentrate around the points in 3 to 7 feet of water, while the giants often take over a prime flat area. When you locate giants, seldom will there be small peacocks in the same spot!

*G*iant peacocks often take to the air after they have exploded on a topwater plug. Other Amazon predators may not be doing a bunch of jumping.

mammals grow to 8 feet long and sport an elongated snout and a pale pink color. Gray dolphins, called "tucuxi" (pronounced "too coo she") in Brazil and "bufeo" in Peru, sometimes follow fishing boats around to reap the benefits of a released, tired and overstressed fish.

Jawbone Action

Unlike almost every other breathing creature in the Amazon, dolphins are not hunted by locals or Indians; rather, they are even fabled and respected. On the other hand, the caiman, due to their meat value, are not. While the black and speckled caiman are now protected in Brazil, there still appear to be thousands of the reptiles in the Uatuma watershed according to our boat's brave nocturnal explorers. With the spots, they spotted numerous caiman eyes within 50 yards of the Clipper each night.

Even during the daylight, Nolan and I noticed several caiman along the river and lagoon banks. One of the most unusual observations of the trip occurred when we were working a small lagoon off the river. Nolan had built a heavy-duty spinnerbait just for the peacock action and was tossing it toward a nondescript bank with only sparse brushy cover at the edge. About 15 feet from the bank, Nolan's rod was almost ripped from his hands.

"It's a grande," shouted my partner, as he fumbled for a modicum of control over the monster. "I can't even turn him. He's a monster. Get the net! Get the net!"

About then, the heavyweight turned and headed for the surface. We expected a giant peacock to explode three feet out of the water as Nolan put all his strength into the bowed heavy-action rod. But there was no explosion. The monster surfaced slowly about 15 feet from the boat and we each did a double-take when two huge jaws full of ragged, pointed teeth opened before us.

Nolan had hooked a 9-foot long caiman on his spinnerbait. Forget the old wife's tail about a gator never feeding below the surface of the water. Prior to the cast, there was no indication of the presence of this reptile in the shallow lagoon. We were both in shock as the battle continued and the caiman again took off.

"Break off," advised our guide using two of his 20-word English vocabulary.

"No, I want my spinnerbait back," bantered Nolan, as though the Indian guide could understand the words, let alone the humor. "You land this gator and get me my lure."

Fortunately for all, the bait pulled free and survived the remarkable ordeal in very good shape. Nolan got a workout and the caiman disappeared, probably a little upset about losing its meal.

Dangerous Liasons

Perhaps the most dangerous (to fishermen) of the exotic rainforest fauna are the freshwater stingrays common throughout the Amazon basin. On previous trips to the Amazon region, I have accidentally hooked a couple of the raya (pronounced "hai ya"). My guide, taking no chances, quickly dispensed of the raya's tail with his machete before unhooking and releasing it.

The catfish of the Uatuma River and other Amazon tributaries are very colorful. The suribim is a relatively common catfish that resembles a black and white canvas with painted hieroglyphic characters. The pintado catfish, sporting a dark, bluish gray back and white sides with black dots all over, grows to over 180 pounds and hits artificial lures with reckless abandon. The cachara catfish has a zebra pattern and the caparari has a tiger pattern with thicker stripes. The pirarara or redtail catfish is a spectacle blending yellow, brown and deep red areas and grows to a couple hundred pounds, as does the jau catfish whose color ranges from a dirty yellow to a black.

The pirarucu reportedly grows to over 10 feet long and to 800 pounds. The tambaqui (pronounced "tom boc key") is a fruit eater that resembles a dark, freshwater drum. They feast below overhanging fruit and nut trees. Our excellent meals aboard the triple-decked Clipper consisted of the bony tambaqui, and the delicious pirarucu and several types of catfish. There are over 3,000 species of fish in the Amazon basin. We just didn't have time to sample them all.

Getting There and Set Up

The logistics of many trips to Brazilian are tough on the body. Lloyd Boliviana Airlines leaves Miami around 9:30 p.m. and arrives in Manaus at 2:30 a.m. which leaves anglers brain-dead as they clear customs and meet up with Gilberto, the Clipper's bilingual camp manager. Over a million people live in the city that was once a frontier town during the rubber boom at the turn of the century.

Just downstream from the airport, the brown water from the Rio Solimoes and the black water of the Rio Negro meet to form the Rio Amazon. The waters, due to different densities and velocities, flow side by side for several miles before mixing, but this is not our fishing destination. After an hour's sleep on a bus, we are transferred about 30 minutes away to the private airport where we board a charter plane and take an hour's flight east to a dirt landing strip at the village of Urucara.

Our group jumped into the back of a flatbed truck and were then driven a mile or so to the Uatuma and the awaiting Clipper. The shallow-draft houseboat motored upstream as we prepared our tackle and ate a light breakfast. Then we boarded the fishing boats and headed off to nearby waters. While fishing during the first and last days of the trip are in waters close to the population centers, the better action is found on days two through the morning of the fifth.

The Amazon Is A Big Deal

The Uatuma River is a minor tributary of the mighty Amazon, which is 4,000 miles long. The Nile is longer, but the Amazon's discharge is 60 times more than the Nile's and in fact, is more than the next eight largest rivers in the world combined! The Amazon has over 7,000 tributaries which drain an area two-thirds the size of the United States. To put the discharge in further perspective, the Amazon contributes 20 percent of all freshwater to the world's oceans.

The Amazon basin contains one-third of the world's remaining rainforest, and its tributaries vary drastically. Some stretch for hundreds and hundreds of miles while others are relatively short. The Uatuma is a mid-length river that has the massive Balbina Reservoir near its headwaters. Productive areas of the Uatuma, like others, vary depending on accessibility to blackwater lagoons and feeder streams which often have the best fishing for peacock. Water levels on the Uatuma and other Amazon tributaries typically control the fishing accessibility, and the watershed's size, water source and topography determine the fluctuations and impact.

In the upper regions of the Uatuma and its lagoons, dense rainforests hemmed in our fishing waters. The Uatuma's most productive blackwater tributaries and lagoons get their tannin-stained colors from acids leeched from forest litter.   Elsewhere in the rainforest, brown water rivers (commonly called whitewater rivers in South America) get their muddy color from suspended sediments carried down from headwaters in the Andes Mountains.   Blue-water tributaries, such as the Rio Tapajos, which flows from the rocky south (of Manaus), are generally clear.

Most of the rainforest's diversity is found high in the treetops. Several million kinds of insects dwell in the forest's upper stories, along with untold numbers of plant and animal species.

For more information on this trip package into the wilds of the Amazon, contact Ron Speed, Jr., Ron Speed's Adventures, 1013 Country Lane, Malakoff, TX 75148; phone (903) 489-1656, fax (903) 489-2856. They also offer excursions to Mexico's hottest bass lake, Huites.

Chapter 5

JUFARI HI-JINKS

Explosive Brazilian action from tropical bass

As the guide nudged the outboard into gear and pointed the bow up the lagoon, I lofted a cast near the small cove that interrupted the rainforest-shrouded bank. We were into our troll just about 20 feet when the attack took place.

My medium-heavy action rod exploded with one of the most astonishing strikes of my life. The giant peacock bass slammed the huge spoon like a train going the other way, and the beefy, 7-foot rod splintered in front of the cork foregrip upon the impact.

My reaction was to grab the remaining 5-foot "section" and point the staff skyward to absorb the powerful charge of the fish as it headed toward some submerged brush near the bank. My efforts to keep the rod tip up were futile, as the monster pulled line from the drag on my firmly attached casting reel. My 60-pound test braid held, but I had more than my hands full trying to combat the awesome peacock.

"Quick Zack," I screamed to my partner, "Grab ahold and help me keep the rod tip up."

Quickly my agile friend jumped over the seat and joined in my fight. As Zack Swanson kept the rod tip section pointed up, I slowly gained back line from a fish that was finally tiring some. Slowly, our team effort pulled the fish toward the boat.

The grand fish jumped three times clearing the surface as we kept tension on the line and prayed. The Pet Spoon's single hook stayed implanted in the fish's jaw and the line and Cross-Lok snap swivel remained intact. Swanson and I were both elated when my guide Sebastiao slid the net under the giant.

We quickly weighed and photographed the destructive fish. The peacock bass weighed 17 1/4 pounds on my partner's small scale.

T.O. McLean was the first angler on the trip to hook a peacock in the upper teens. He had just started his troll with a giant topwater plug when the giant hit it.

Swanson, Sales Manager for VMC hooks, pointed out that the hook in the Luhr-Jensen spoon was a 6/0 VMC brand as we took pictures of the fish, the bait and the broken rod. That big fish was my first and most exciting action that day in the Jufari River system in northern Brazil.

Swanson also caught his two biggest peacocks of the week that day. The twins weighed 14 1/4 pounds each and came from two different lagoons. We caught several others up to 12 1/2 pounds in the blackwater lakes off the Amazon tributary.

The week in the rainforest was a very successful one for me. I caught two monsters, one 20 and the other 22 pounds, and eight other "teeners" during the week, but none of them shattered my rod. My equipment fared well in the four great lakes that I found that week. My guide and I searched some 25 different waters to find the deeper lakes that held the giants. Friend T.O. McLean actually beat me into one of them on day two.

I had quickly caught a five pound peacock from the mouth of a lagoon when I heard a voice from behind the trees separating the main water body from the "boca".

"Want to photograph a big fish?," he asked. "I caught an 18-pounder as I started to troll my Woodchopper."

Needless to say, we rounded the point of trees and got our photos. The fish measured 32 inches and was released in healthy condition. It was the same lake where two days later I caught a 34-inch long 20-

A smashing strike as the author trolled a number 18 Pet Spoon resulted in a broken rod and 19 plus pounds of belligerent peacock. Larry caught three over 20 pounds that week which didn't break his rod!

pounder. In fact, I caught and released three other giants in those waters. That lake was adjacent to an even better "secret" lake, as host Rodolfo Fernandez and guide Sebastiao Ferreira Brito called it.

Secrets Revealed

Our secret lake held even more giants and was much smaller. Brito discovered it from the lay of the horizon, and Fernandez, an expert fly fisherman, and I checked it out early in the week. The circular lagoon dropped off quickly into 30 feet of water. The super-deep lake was a caster's lake, too small to even consider trolling. My Woodchoppers explored every part of the surface over a five-hour period, but my partner started off with his fly rod.

Within an hour after discovering the lagoon, Fernandez caught a giant, 25-inch long butterfly peacock that weighed over 8 pounds and had a 15 inch girth. The fish struck one of Fernandez' hand-tied creations that he calls the "Ariramba Fly". My action soon followed. On a Peacock Bass colored Big Game Woodchopper and the silver Pet Spoon that day, I caught 11 over 10 pounds, including two 15 pounders and my 22 pounder (which also measured 34 inches). The latter fish struck at 11:30 a.m. Fernandez caught his biggest fish of the week an hour later after switching to conventional casting equipment and a Woodchopper, and it weighed 15 pounds.

As expected, those two lakes cooled on my second and third attempts to enjoy their bounty. I and my partner could count on one or two giants from the previously "red-hot holes". My clown pattern Woodchopper cast to deep, open waters paid off handsomely early in the week, but a trolled Number 18 Pet Spoon was responsible for several giants the last half of the week.

Overall, though, I had a very good week on the Rio Jufari, tallying 124 peacocks that included 28 fish over 10 pounds. My best "numbers" day was 32, but my catch each day was double-digit. My second and third full days on the waters were best in terms of giants, or "teeners", with three each. During the week, I caught two 13-pounders, five 15-pounders, one 17-pounder, two 19-pounders and the two over 20 pounds.

Friends Join In The Bounty

Friends, Andrew Taylor and his brother, John, had productive weeks as well catching fish up to 20 pounds. Andrew heads up Stamina Fishing Lure Components which sells hooks, split rings, screw eyes and fly-tying materials through a consumer catalog. For those wanting to obtain hardware to modify their lures, he can be reached at 800-546-8922. Drew Butterwick of Linn, Texas joined me on our last day in camp and caught his largest peacock, a 15 pounder, while trolling one of my Big Game Woodchoppers.

When he is not working in the Brazilian Amazonas region, our camp host, Fernandez, lives on the banks of the "river of the painted birds" as the Rio Uruguay near Montevideo, Uruguay, is known. While he has fished other Amazon tributaries extensively, this was his first trip to the Rio Jufari.

My friendly guide for the week was perhaps the Amazon's best non-English-speaking fishing guide. I've probably fished with more than 75 guides in the Amazon, and Brito's personally was the best. He worked

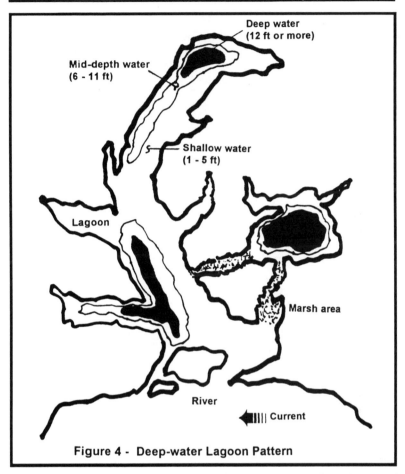

Figure 4 - Deep-water Lagoon Pattern

Figure 4 - There are a lot of lagoons off the Jufari River, but in general, only the handful of deeper ones are those that offer excellent peacock fishing for giant fish. Both casting and trolling the deeper stretches when waters are low will locate the concentrations of giant peacocks. This deep-water lagoon pattern is the most productive strategy for such areas. You may have to check depth a lot to discover the better waters, unless you can relay your wishes precisely to your guide - assuming he is intimately familiar with the waters being fished

hard and kept the long, hot days very interesting with his attempts at learning English, his joking and laughter.

I communicated with him in "Portunol", a combination of Portuguese and Spanish which helps me "get by" when in the rainforest. He asked questions about translations and comfortably addressed me by my first name, a rarity for any of my previous guides. His one wish was to be "famous" - to be mentioned in one of my books. He did a good job helping me locate peacock and positioning the boat so that I could effectively fish them, so his performance definitely warrants such an acknowledgement.

Jungle Atmosphere

There are lots of water birds along the Rio Jufari, including giant storks, kingfishers flying from tree to tree along the meandering waterway, hawks, egrets and multi-colored herons. On this trip I noticed more indigenous ducks puddling around and more terns constantly diving on schools of minnows than I have seen on any other rainforest waters. Several other species of birds including scarlet ibis, macaws, parrots and parakeets were sighted.

We also saw otters and a couple of "jacare" or caiman. Capybara, sloth, and even monkeys are sometimes seen around lakes and lagoons of the Jufari. In the waters swimming with peacock bass are many species of fish with awesome teeth, freshwater stingrays and dolphin, and many other varieties of colorful forage fish.

In fact, we came across some of the tropical fish netters in one area of the river. They had set out containment or "holding" nets for their stock. Much of the discus, tetras and other colorful exotic freshwater aquarium fish are collected in the tributaries around Barcelos. The Rio Negro town with a population of about 7,000, is called the "tropical aquarium fish capital of the world".

The tropical fish catchers are native river people, called "caboclos" who pack in supplies at Barcellos and then, with their families, slowly motor the 50 miles or so upstream to the Jufari River area where we were fishing. They travel in creaky, overloaded houseboats once the rainy season is over. They eke out a living from the rivers flowing into the Rio Negro.

From primitive fishing camps, some also hunt turtles with traps scattered around in lagoons. They use low-riding dugout canoes and catch food fish with their handlines. They also dab feathered lures from cane-type poles in brushy areas along the banks as they scull the dugout with their free hand. And, they do quite well catching sport fish.

T op guide honors may go to Sebastiao Ferreira Brito who adeptly handled all my big peacocks from the Rio Jufari area. I called him "Mr. Personality".

As waters rise to make navigation again less hazardous and their harvest peaks, they head downstream to their villages and rainy season quarters. When not on the water during the dry season, they can be found scattered along the banks of the Negro living in stilted houses setting on tiny patches of cleared land from the rainforest.

Safari Camp

Our accommodations for the week were mobile, floating camps, called "Jungalows". The comfortable two-person tent barges are on 10 foot by 15 foot platforms, each with toilet, river shower, sink facilities, lights, ventilation fans, table and chair. They have fully screened walls, carpeting, canvas roof and an aluminum entry door. The main screened-in lodge barge has a lounge area and bar situated on the river bank and usually adjoining a white sand beach.

The aluminum-hulled barges draw just a few inches of water, ideal for mobility in shallow waters. The floating camp, which is normally parked on a sand beach, only travels safely at up to 3 miles per hour in

Rodolfo Fernandez, camp host, took great care in releasing the numerous giants that he and I caught from the Jufari.

low winds and moderate current, so moving it is a slow process. That sometimes occurs between groups of fishermen to the camp.

The safari camp accommodates up to 8 anglers per week during the low-water "season". Luis Brown, owner of the River Plate Anglers operation, offers purified water (not bottled water) and daily maid/ laundry service. "Roughing it" in this safari camp is not really difficult.

The camp's narrow-hulled fishing craft are 18-foot aluminum boats with 40 h.p. outboards, ideal to easily traverse the waterscape of the more remote tributaries. They can access the numerous "furos" or backwater river channels and the "igarapies" or narrow creeks that parallel the main river.

On The Move

Outfitter Brown actually has two active mobile camps on remote regions of the Amazon watershed that are distant from other fishing pressure. Scott Swanson of Quest is the U.S. booking agent for this trip to the Jufari. For the adventurous angler who enjoys getting off the beaten path, this trip is hard to beat.

T *ravel to the floating camp from a nearby landing trip is often via*
amphibious or float plane. The mobile camp can be moved in a day
or so to new waters, if the need arises.

"Brown's fly-in operation often puts you on smaller tributaries that
can be accessed via shallow-draft boats or, in some cases, only by float
plane," explains Swanson. "He uses aerial observation to locate prime
fishing areas. The remote waters often lie above natural boating barriers
such as shallow river mouth sandbars."

Guests normally fly overnight into Manaus from Miami and then
connect with a charter flight to a smaller airport near the more remote

---

Running The River

When I first laid eyes on the Jufari River, it was about two days after my guide had first
laid his eyes on it. He had not been on the water before, so, in effect, we were both
exploring the massive waterway. Experience definitely comes into play when moving
through unknown waters.

There are certain keys to "running a river" successfully without hitting a lot of sand bars.
Here are some of the clues which indicate current and a deeper river channel when it all
seems like a maze of shallow waters separated by numerous islands and flooded marsh.
Knowing what to look for will help keep navigation safe and maximize the fishing time.

     1. riffles over sand bars,
     2. movement of aquatic grass,
     3. high banks,
     4. taller, larger trees,
     5. wakes off small limbs,
     6. sandy, shallow inner bends,
     7. debris in trees from higher waters,
     8. bubbles,
     9. fallen trees,
    10. eroded banks,
    11. sharp slopes,
    12. leaf movement,
    13. oxbow direction with inner-bend bushes and outside deeper banks.

waters. From there, an amphibious or float plane takes them to the camp. The watershed being fished depends on its water level.

While we were on the Jufari River, the Rio Matupiri and Rio Marmelos, both tributaries of the Rio Madeira, are favorites of Brown. The two peacock-laden rivers to the south of Manaus run hundreds of miles offering numerous lagoons along their length.   Much of the surrounding area are "igapos" or portions of land that are permanently inundated with water much of their life. The Pan'ra (pronounced "pon ha") Indians have dry season campsites on the igapos below the better fishing on the Marmelos.

Weather can affect most areas of the Amazon, and the Matupiri and Marmelos are no exception. In the dry season, natural and man-made fires may burn unchecked due to lack of rain. El Nino in late 1997 left many lagoons off the Matupiri high and dry in the dry season from August through December. In such low waters, peacocks retreat to the rocks and depth of the river channel. They hang out near stream inlets and below rapids in quieter waters.

Other choices of Brown's include the Rio Caures (pronounced "cow race") which flows through the rich jungles south of Barcellos and the Rio Tapara (Itapara) whose clear waters twist and bend southward through the state of Roraima. The Tapara flows through narrow forest-canopied passages on its ways to a juncture with the Rio Branco. The current in the Tapara speeds around islands and through cuts and then slows through blackwater lagoons.

One of Brown's newest finds for one of his base of operations is the Macucuau River which has expansive sand flats and small, quiet lagoons nearby. The River Plate owner/operator has also offered trips on the Amazon Goddess riverboat for up to 10 anglers. They often run at night and the droning engine generally lulls you to sleep.

River Plate angling adventures are also extensively covered in chapter 3 of "Peacock Bass & Other Fierce Exotics". For more information on this River Plate Angling fishing safari, contact Scott Swanson at Quest, 3595 Canton Hwy., Ste. #C11, Marietta, GA 30066, or phone (888) 891-3474.

Chapter 6

VENTUARI VITALS

Key on rock gardens and land-locked lagoons in Venezuela's Amazonas State

I had just finished my usual opening remarks to my fishing partner - the ones about using a "team approach" to cast to any feeding fish or activity noticed behind a hooked fish in hopes of catching a "double." Captain Frank Ibarra nodded as he set the hook into a leaping peacock.

His fish had just landed back in the water when my lure splashed down two feet away. I didn't even have a chance to twitch the topwater bait. A second peacock exploded on it, and I set back on the rod.

"That's exactly what I meant," I proclaimed, as the 10 pounder set off on an aerial display of his own.

We both worked our fish to boat and noticed each had another or two following along. Schools of peacock are like that. Often, the competitive fish will follow hooked fish and strike at any nearby offering. That's often true, but to "double" on our first cast was an exciting start to the day.

I was fishing the Ventuari River with Ibarra, General Manager of Manaka Jungle Lodge in the Venezuelan state of Amazonas. Ibarra is an excellent angler with extensive knowledge of the peacock bass and other species found in the river and lagoons. With very accurate casting, we caught another four or five doubles that day and ended up with about 20 peacock bass overall. The following day's tallies were in the 20 peacock per boat range on the waters that were still high from winter rains.

Located 420 miles south of Caracas at the confluence of the Orinoco and Ventuari rivers, Manaka Jungle Lodge is surrounded by a carpet of dense jungle and jutting, table-topped mountains called "tepuis". The massive pillars of bedrock sometimes spawn clear black waterfalls that plunge hundreds of feet into a gorge at their base.

There are numerous scenic "tepuis" or table-topped mountains near the confluence of the Orinoco and Ventuari rivers in southern Venezuela.

Manaka Jungle Lodge, on the Orinoco/Ventuari river system delta, offers a vast fishing area, and a strict peacock bass catch-and-release policy. From the lodge, anglers can fish a stretch of the Orinoco that flows in from the south, or they can go westward upstream on the Ventuari. Rocky outcropping exists on both beautiful rivers, but only a few lagoons are found off each.

For those who prefer to fish only for peacock bass and want large numbers of fish, you can expect fairly long boat rides to the few nutrient-rich lagoons. The fish are less structure-oriented and tend to wander throughout the lagoons searching for food. The closest lagoon is located about 45 minutes from camp, but most of them are approximately an hour away. Yellow macaws often scold boaters from the skies as they move from one spot to another.

With guide Alexis, Ibarra and I walked through the jungle into a couple of land-locked lagoons where a small aluminum boat was waiting. Alexis mounted the trolling motor and we began working the flooded banks. The water levels in the isolated lakes were also very high and the fishing was off a little, but we managed to catch about 25 from one and 15 from another a day later. The water color was off, but both lagoons showed potential for great low-water fishing later in the season.

Our visit to one lagoon far up the Ventuari River ran into another type of problem. You often find this in the river-accessible lagoons: pestering fresh water porpoise. The mammals tend to follow the boats in hopes of picking off an easy meal. That sometimes turns off the peacocks and limits success.

Rockbound Gardening

Ibarra and I fished some of the unique rock gardens and caught both peacock bass and payara. The size of the peacocks in the riverine area

A land-locked lagoon off the Orinoco River yielded this 12 1/2 pound peacock to Frank Ibarra. It slammed a large Luhr-Jensen Pet Spoon. There were no "teeners" to be had on this trip, and I'm sure that the high water - up some 6 feet from normal - had a lot to do with it. I did get a report that one angler had caught a 22 pounder from one of the lagoons two weeks earlier.

was significant. In fact, I personally caught several between 8 and 11 pounds from the rock eddies. The big fish of our three day activity were a two peacocks that each weighed 12 1/2 pounds. Ibarra and I caught them in one of the land-locked lakes off the Orinoco that we walked into.

The Ventuari is known for its numbers of mid-size peacock and its variety, not for its giant peacocks. Some of the rock gardens in the central river channels are located slightly closer to camp, but the best may be up to an hour away. Here, the angler has a much more diverse variety of species to choose from, yet can still expect to catch 10 or 15 peacock a day. Reportedly, some fish over 20 pounds have been taken over the years from rock gardens within 30 minutes of camp!

When fishing the rock gardens in the central channel, the fisherman should have two different rods set up. One for the toothy game fish, such as payara and piranha, usually found in current on the upstream side of rocks and which should be fished with a 6-inch steel leader.

The second rod should be rigged with a topwater lure to be thrown into the cracks and crevices on the downstream side of the rocks for the peacock bass. You can also expect a breakoff or two due to the sharp rocks that a bully peacock might run into.

Massive rock gardens in the rivers yield peacock bass from the eddies and payara from the current runs. Accuracy is important because peacock bass hold right against the rocks. You can expect lots of fish to come up and engulf your plug.

Other commonly-caught species in the river include the payara, which has two very impressive canine teeth and a mouth full of menacing dentures and a couple of species of piranha. Other possible species that you may catch include catfish, sardinata (which resembles a giant shad), morocoto (a large bluegill-type fish that reaches 30 pounds), guabina or traira, and many other exotic fish. Most anglers will be surprised at how hard these species in the Ventuari and Orinoco hit a lure, the power and tenacity of their fight, and how much they jump.

Seasonal Satisfaction

Manaka Jungle Lodge is located approximately 150 miles north of the equator, so the fairly constant daytime temperatures ranges between 85 and 95 degrees. There is moderate humidity and typically a refreshing breeze coming off the river. The fishing season coincides with the dry season, January through mid-April, so the weather should be sunny with only an occasional rain shower.

This trip offers anglers beautiful scenery in the form of rock gardens, river currents, islands, and the tepuis or table top mountains. The water is never rough, and the only biting insects are "no-see-ums", which can be a nuisance during the early part of the season. Long pants, long-sleeve shirts, and a good bug spray help dissuade them effectively. After sundown, there are few biting insects.

Oasis of Comfort

Manaka Jungle Lodge was built in the middle of the Amazonas jungle in 1987. Still, today the nearest place to find construction materials is a three-day boat ride. Anglers reside in one of six very comfortable "churuatas" (or individual bungalows) that are designed to

The Manaka Lodge was built in the middle of the Amazonas jungle, yet it offers excellent service in addition to very comfortable accommodations.

conform to the native architecture of the Baniba and Piaroa Indians. Each roomy churuata contains two twin beds with overhead fans, a private bath and a large porch with hammock. There is daily maid and laundry service available.

A separate, spacious dining and lounging area is a popular spot to relax and tell a few stories at the end of day. Or you can just sit back and watch satellite TV, while the chef prepares continental and national dishes composed of fresh fruits and vegetables, plus fish, beef and chicken. The lodge has plenty of bottled water, 24-hour electricity, a satellite telephone, and ice for the coolers.

The new fishing boats at the lodge are Bass Trackers with 40 hp outboards. They are very comfortable fishing rigs with live wells, bilge pump, storage, and are suitable for both lagoons and the river. Each has a trolling motor and batteries here are full of charge. The guides have nets in the boat, but I prefer to save them for use only on giant peacocks.

If you would like to explore the jungle and learn about its people, the staff are glad to spend a day showing off the birds, wildlife, and fascinating Indian cultures that live in the surrounding areas. They can take you into the Baniba and Piaroa villages to view their interesting lifestyles, or wander along a jungle trail to learn about how the Indians utilize the forest for medicine, food, and building materials.

Much of the wildlife is very reclusive and usually nocturnal in the Amazon, but you might see tapirs, capybara, monkeys, jaguar, river otters and other jungle animals. You will see fresh water porpoise in the lagoons and river and numerous parrots and colorful macaws, toucans, ibis, herons, osprey, orioles, and migrating shorebirds. Obviously, the heavier concentrations of birdlife are found in the more remote areas.

A young macaw perched on Ibarra's shoulder enjoys the camp atmosphere and food.   Most parrots in the area, however, are confined to the forested canopies along the river.

Rocky Rollicks

The Ventuari is a favorite river of avid peacock basser Greg Margerum. The angler has often caught numerousf fish averaging 8 or 9 pounds, and in fact, his largest "pavon", an 18 pounder, came on a trip to Manaka Jungle Lodge. He was fishing from a huge boulder in the river while his guide, Orlando, overlooked the action perched on an even larger rock.

Margerum hooked the fish on a medium light spinning rod and reel and 10 pound test Trilene Big Game. He chased the hooked fish from one rock pool to another as the guide laughed. After 20 minutes both angler and fish ran out of steam. They landed, weighed and revived the fish before releasing it. Margerum and his partner each hooked and lost an even bigger peacock, thanks to a broken rod, in one case, and a sharp rock, in the other.

A sharp rock also separated me from a big fish on the Ventuari during my trip. Even heavy line can succumb to the ragged edge of such habitat. The peacock are mostly hiding behind the big rocks that block the current, and in many such places, they are concentrated. It is not unusual to catch five or six peacocks between 8 and 12 pounds from a "honey hole" right in the river out of the current.

Additional information on Orinoco tributaries also exist in my book, "Peacock Bass Explosions". For more information on the comfortable trip, contact Captain Frank Ibarra, Manaka Jungle Lodge, 7300 NW 34th Street, Miami, FL 33122; phone 011-582-979-2796, fax 011-582-978-1230, or e-mail "franibar834@cantv.net".

Chapter 7

PERUVIAN TREASURES

Exploring the Amazon headwaters for eco-enjoyment

Peru offers a unique opportunity for anglers wanting to experience the upper Amazon and its ecotourism facets. Howard McKinney of Fishabout has been taking anglers to Peru for the past eight years. The U.S. agent has literally fished all over that country with some successes and some failures.

I fished with him recently in waters off the Rio Tigre which lie southwest of the "largest Indian village" in the world, Iquitos. From the double-decker "Amazon Explorer" houseboat, we explored some new areas that had not previously been fished by sportfishermen. Unfortunately, the water in the river and lagoons was still high from the rainy season and the fishing was off that week.

A couple of dozen peacocks averaging about 3 1/2 pounds and a like number of other exotics were my bounty, but memories from angling with an enjoyable group of Californians were "keepers." In addition to the peacock which ranged from about one to 8 pounds, I landed some primitive trieda which are called "fasaco" or "wolf fish" in Peru. Bicuda, sabalo, piranha, small payara called "chambira", and cachorra or payara as they are commonly known, were among my other catches in the four day exploratory. I also caught a 6-barred cichlid that resembled an elongated perch that is called a "bocachica".

We were up and out fishing by 6:30 or 7:00 each morning and back to the boat by 10:30 or 11:00 for a late breakfast. Then we normally waited around for lunch and went back out around 2:00 or 2:30 p.m. We fished until 5:00 or 5:30 p.m. in small aluminum fishing boats or paddle-powered, square stern canoes. Two anglers plus a guide were in the former, while the freeboard of the latter insured only one angler with the guide.

The lightweight boats in our armada were often carried overland to small landlocked lakes where the guides paddled our 10 anglers along typically brush-laden shorelines. A few boats were powered by small outboards and they could run up small channels into the estuaries and lagoons. Several small villages dotted the riverbank and giggling children typically gathered on the shoreline when we anchored nearby in the evening.

My biggest peacock was about 8 pounds, but a monster paiche (arapaima) of about 200 pounds was taken by Jorge, a local "angler" who was showing us some new water. He speared the giant fish. I saw monkeys in the trees, but very few big peacock bass on this trip. "Exploratories" are like that. You may hit it big or find very little to write about. Fortunately, McKinney's vast experience in the wilds of Peru are noteworthy.

Maranon Missions

"The first year we started fishing out of Iquitos, we would run upstream from Iquitos to the intersection of the Maranon and the Ucayali," says McKinney. "These two rivers form the Amazon River just south of Iquitos."

"One of the small tributaries there, a river called the Yarapa, had four very good lakes that we fished," he continues. "We really didn't have to go much farther than that then. One of the nearby lakes was Aguajal, which is where another Peru fishing operation, Camp Peacock, was located in its early years."

McKinney's biggest peacock from Peruvian waters was taken from a lake very near to Iquitos. He was fishing a little lake in a borrowed eight-foot-long dugout canoe next to an Indian village off the Rio Tahuayo. His catch, a golden peacock with three black bars and some irregular splotches, was reportedly 11 or 12 pounds.

"Like most of our peacock bass catches, the big one was taken on a Rat-L-Trap," says McKinney. "A 3/4-ounce chrome with blue back would be my choice, if I could use one lure."

The Yarapa and its quebradas or creeks, are often blackwater and so are most of the region's lakes. The lagoons along the Yarapa were mostly unattached to the river (or landlocked) at low water. The boats had to be dragged about 50 yards or so to the small lakes, according to McKinney. The Aguajal Lake was connected for most of the dry period.

Many of the fishing boats used by the "Amazon Explorer" operation were small and paddle-powered.

"That's the farthest we had to go then to find some fairly good peacock bass fishing," says the avid peacock basser. "What happened was, we started looking farther not only because we were looking for better fishing - we've always been looking for the best fishing - but also because the pressure from Iquitos and the commercial fishermen started to move upriver."

As pressure increased, McKinney moved his operation farther away from Iquitos, a huge village of 500,000 population and a major trading center. The jungle-surrounded Indian village is located in the heart of the upper Amazon River rain forest, some 2,300 miles upstream from the city of Belem, Brazil at the Atlantic Ocean and some 750 air miles from the Pacific Ocean. It is where all the Peruvian fishing operations embark.

There are once a week flights from Miami to Iquitos (currently on Saturdays). McKinney's Fishabout clients are transferred by floatplane to the houseboat on day two. They use both the "Amazon Explorer" and the 65-foot "Delfin" on occasion. The showers are cool river waters which can be cold, but the Explorer's cabins are air conditioned for hot times in the jungle. At night, the steady chug of the engine is like a sleeping pill. After four full days of fishing, anglers board a "speedboat taxi" and take a very long boat ride (7 hours) back to Iquitos.

Tiger Tracks

"We then moved our operation farther up the Maranon and fished the next two years near where the Rio Tigre flows into the big river," says McKinney. "We found good quality fishing there near Nueve Miraflores in an area called San Pablo Tapischa. We caught large quantities of three- to five-pound peacock bass in the black water lake."

Although, the lake yielded some big catches, it received heavy commercial fishing pressure, because a navigable channel goes right into it," says McKinney. "We were there in late September and the peacocks were in the shallows spawning. The big males had the great big bulbous nob. We were actually fishing right alongside the guys that were netting, and at the time we felt like we were showing the netters where the peacocks were."

"Just downstream was the little village of Soltrito and a landlocked lake that was about a half a mile long," he continues. "It was very deep and very black, and we had some very good fishing for peacock bass up to 10 pounds in that lake. There was another lake that was a 15-minute walk through Soltrito and another 45-minute walk into a tiny lake that also had peacock bass and a variety of species."

"Our plans were to go up into an area called the Picaya Samiria which is a protected park," McKinney says. "We had gotten permits to go farther up the Samiria River through four check stations, but when we got in that area, we found that the lakes were too shallow. It was a great wildlife area; we had never seen so much wildlife, so many birds and monkeys, but the depth of the water was not conducive to peacock bass."

"Then, we moved up the Rio Tigre to the blackwater tributary called Rio Nahuapa near the town of Miraflores," McKinney says. "We fished a couple lakes there, including one called Mission, that produced well for a couple of years. Then, we moved farther up the Tigre to a blackwater lake called Changa Cocha where there was some really quality fishing for awhile."

"Our hopes were high because that was the farthest we've gone up the Tigre," explains McKinnney. "There are numerous quebradas off the river, but in this particular case, the water was high. We also found some of the same netting pressures that we've found in other lakes. I'm told a couple of the lakes turned on and produced well the week after our trip."

Napo Cochas

"In our third year, we traveled up the Rio Napo to a village called Pueblo Mazan and fished four or five remote lakes off the small Mazan River," he continues. "The main lake in the middle of the jungle called Tigre Cocha had good fishing for peacocks and even yielded a 20-pound paiche to a Rat-L-Trap. We could only go up a certain distance there, but at the time, it served us well."

The Rio Mazan is a blackwater river that flows into the Napo right above the Napo's confluence with the Amazon. FishAbout clients reportedly also caught payara and paiche on the Mazan. Near the mouth of the Napo where it flows into the Amazon is another good fishing place called Atun Cocha. It is supposedly the lake that the president of Peru likes to fish.

"We have also fished an area called Curaray that's a tributary off the Napo," McKinney says. "We found numerous lakes that were still high

Howard McKinney, showing off a mid-size Peruvian peacock, has explored many of the waters in the Upper Amazon region. On my trip with McKinney, we explored a handful of lakes further upstream on the Tigre River around the village of Intuto and above it almost to Aucsurco. Intuto lies near the tributary Corrientes River, an area with clusters of palms along some banks.

in August, and locals told us that their low waters occurred in December and January which kind of surprised me. Even at high water, we caught a dozen fish, and I think that area has some potential."

Yavari Yarns

"While exploring this country, I have fished the Rio Yavari which flows into the 'three frontiers' area where Colombia, Peru and Brazil come together," says McKinney. "It runs along the Peru/Brazil border downstream from Iquitos and offers some good fishing. I've sent expeditions as far as 200 miles up the Yavari and some were very successful."

There are numerous blackwater lagoons on the Yavari and its tributaries, but the downstream portion has experienced fishing pressure from the town of Leticia. In 1997, McKinney flew there and spent a week exploring an area called Colonia Angamos, which is close to the headwaters of the Rio Yavari at the confluence of the Rio Galvez.

"We went up the area's rivers, but didn't really get very far," admits McKinney. "We ran into the same sort of snafus you find traveling around other parts of the third world due to poor planning. Overall, we weren't really too impressed with the mostly shallow lakes which seemed to have populations nearby that affected them."

If a person is brave enough to fly to, and fish, the Rio Putumayo on the border of Colombia, there may be some good fishing in the lakes there, according to McKinney. Some outfitters in Peru also visit the Rio Orosa region which includes blackwater lakes or "cochas", jungle streams and pools and whitewater rivers. The Yacumama Lodge, located on the Yarapa River, reportedly offers a balance between a total wilderness experience and personal comfort and some peacock fishing for fish up to 7 or 8 pounds. Camp Peacock currently flies anglers out of Iquitos on a turbo prop float plane to Cajacuma where their Boatel is now located. The flying time is a little over one hour.

Timing The Bite

"I think that I've probably seen as much of Peru's peacock bass fishing as any other person in my business," he adds. "I've looked hard and long and spent a lot of money. I continue to find reasonably good fishing for fish up to 10 or 12 pounds, but I have not found really big fish. I have had larger fish lost at the boat, but on an average the fish are four to five pounds."

The best months to fish Peru are from July through September. July is sometimes a little early and September sometimes is a little late. August can be considered the middle of the season.

Parts of the Peruvian Amazon have a 30 to 40 foot water level rise each year during the rainy season, and river waters overflow banks in the floodplain. Fish move into the flooded rainforest and become scarce. When waters return to dry season levels, the peacocks find lagoons or quebradas to again take up residence.

The Iquitos guides that FishAbout has been using over the past several years seem to know how to judge how far a person can cast and keep him that distance from shore. They do a good job and work extra hard especially when you take into account that in many lakes that they fish, boats have to be dragged up mud banks and through jungle lowlands to the water. The anglers then walk in and fish them, and if the lakes don't fish well, the guides drag the boats out again, and move on.

About 50 percent of the lakes that are fished are landlocked and the walk is between about 5 minutes and 20 minutes. You don't have to be an athlete to walk through the jungle, but you may have to climb up a muddy bank or walk a plank from the boat to shore.

Night Nature Walks/Other Interests

"I think that Peru provides a far more interesting trip for the traveling angler than many of the other locations just because of the

Paiche are the largest specie of fish swimming in the Amazon watershed, and they are usually netted or speared by the Indians of Peru. If you're looking to beat the netters to the fish, it's best to be there right as the water drops, according to McKinney.

friendliness of the people, the villages, the characters of the rivers themselves, and the way we do it," he says. "We sometimes hike in the jungle and go out at night looking for creatures and animals. There's a lot of fun things that go on in the town of Iquitos itself."

"Peru is an excellent adventure fishing destination," continues the California agent. "However, when I sell the trip, I'm really careful to let people know that this is a lot more than just a fishing trip. At times, we have very good fishing for peacocks up to 10 pounds and other times, we have to look around for fish. We're always looking around for lakes in the jungle, and we always have a good time."

"The typical customer interested in this type of trip is one that has an equal interest in coming to see the Amazon and to experience the entire trip," McKinney explains. "It's a fishing adventure more than anything else. There are times when we have excellent fishing and there are times when we have tough fishing. However, it's always an interesting

Towing fishing boats behind a double-decker houseboat is about the only way to explore the remote upper Rio Amazon region.

trip because we have night expeditions in the jungle. A guide that is well versed in the flora and fauna accompanies the hike."

"We also stop in river villages and visit and trade with the extremely friendly and curious Indians which adds to the whole adventure," he continues. "It is not strictly a fishing trip. If somebody calls and says they're going to evaluate the quality of this trip simply by the number of fish they catch, I will usually steer them in another direction towards something that's more of a cut and dry fishing-type program."

"Each one of our rain forest expeditions has a guide aboard who is into herpetology, dolphin studies, bird watching, flora and fauna, and natural history," he adds. "The activities two or three times a week really enhance the trip. They may find boas or anacondas in the trees or creeks, as well as some unique beetles, insects and birds. This is fishing in the morning and evening, a nice relaxing river trip and an interesting Amazon adventure."

Part of the adventure there may also include biting bugs. In the brownwater areas, they can be bad. I kept well-oiled with insect lotion and wore long sleeve shirts and long pants and socks the entire time to minimize the no-seeum welts.

Water aboard the "Amazon Explorer" is safe to drink, but anywhere in South America, it is always wise to watch carefully what you eat. I usually avoid ice, thin skinned fruits, uncooked vegetables and salads.

Other Peru adventures are presented in my book, "Peacock Bass & Other Fierce Exotics". When traveling to Peru, it is wise to consult your physician or a local Travel Medicine Clinic concerning shots or pills you may need. Up to date information can also be obtained by calling the Center for Disease Control at 1-404-332-4559.

Chapter 8

THE MYSTERIOUS XINGU

Golden peacocks swim with giant crocodile perch and other exotics

The surface explosion was a "giveaway." I noticed a broad tail with the signature "peacock eye" kicking water skyward. The yellowish fish with the bright yellow-haloed black spot was indeed a peacock bass and an aggressive one. Are there any other kind?

An extremely irritated eight pounder moved in and out of the water across the tiny slough. It swam into and out of some submerged branches and then went around some fallen rocks on the shoreline just 20 feet away. Careful pressure led the fish out of its rockpile, and soon my partner grabbed the fish with his fish pliers.

I marveled at its coloration, a vivid golden color with tiny black flecks similar to those found on the freshwater golden dorado whose range is several hundred miles to the south. I have not seen peacocks with such colors in any of my travels to their many homes. That was my first one of the trip and I caught several more with the same "painting".

I also caught and released several others sporting more conventional markings plus some with random black splotches across their bodies. Regardless of coloration, they generally weighed between 4 and 8 pounds, typical for the Rio Xingu watershed. Several of my peacocks were taken from the Bau, a small stream that is also full of "crocodile perch", as Russ Clement of the Xingu Lodge, affectionately calls the traira or dogfish.

In fact, right after landing the 8 pound peacock, I caught a 10 pound crocodile perch about 20 feet down the bank. Then, in the following 20 casts, I hooked and landed eight more of the ugly creatures. I caught another two peacocks that afternoon in the tiny creek and finished out with three more toothy crocodile perch. My largest was a 17 pounder

Russ Clement of the Xingu Lodge with one of the Rio Xingu's golden peacock bass. A topwater plug fooled this lagoon-based fish.

which tore up the waterway and my Rat-L-Trap's hooks, but I was able to land it.

Anglers who want to experience the real wilds of the Amazon rain forest don't have to look further than the Xingu. The clear, boulder-strewn currents are loaded with a variety of big fish, such as the ugly trieda, big payara or "cachorra" up to about 25 pounds and even, in some areas big peacock bass.

The 2,200-mile long Xingu flows from south in the Brazilian state of Mato Grosso northward through the state of Para where it joins the Amazon River south of the town of Altamira. The Xingu cascades through 16 major rapids, and its largest tributary, the Iriri, is a 1,250-mile long river with 12 significant rapids. The other branching tributaries of the mysterious Xingu include the Liberdade, Riozinho, Triunfo, Bacaja, Fresco, and Curua, and all have numerous rapids.

Surrounded by virgin forest, the upper end of Xingu flows serenely north. There are several lagoons in that area, but much of the beautiful river flows through deep valleys cut through the Brazilian Highlands. The Xingu there, with its fast water, midstream boulders, turbulent rapids, rocky islands, and deep, tranquil pools offers excellent fishing for a variety of species.

Big sportfish live in the forest-shrouded waterways, and here you may catch a world record traira, piranha, bicuda, or possibly cachorra. The optimal fishing times and conditions in the northern areas are from September to December and in the southern areas, from May to October.

Fifth World Peacocks

"The fishery here is primarily riverine in nature," says Clement. "Peacocks are lying behind huge rocks off the rapids, in tiny sloughs off

The author landed this toothy 17-pound "crocodile perch" or traira. The prehistoric fish is a tremendous fighter with its thick, wide tail. Crocodile perch in the Xingu River region grow to 25 pounds and pound for pound, they are tremendous fighters with their thick, wide tails being a match for any sportsman. They are a blast to catch. On one day, a couple of visitors to Clement's lodge caught 200 of them on Bau Creek and the Bom Jardin, a tiny creek on the other side of the Xingu.

the twisting channel, behind islands and in small cuts in the rocky banks. But most any cast may result in a surprise catch."

This is one trip where anglers must forgo comfort in order to explore and fish the edge of civilization, . On one fall trip a couple of years ago, I found the fishing good, but there were many biting bugs and primitive accommodations. Even Clement calls the isolated and primitive Xingu River surroundings, including the village of Sao Felix do Xingu, the "Fifth World."

The largest peacock reportedly taken from that area of the Xingu has been 18 pounds, but Clement has seen others over 15. He has also seen peacocks sporting a variety of designs. The number of stripes or bars on each side may vary from three to as much as a dozen, according to the operator. The most beautiful are those with no stripes and simply entirely golden sides, as was the one described above

*T*he Xingu watershed is a beautiful place that is visited by few "outsiders." Indians still paddle the fish-laden currents, and the few outposts along the way are at the edge of civilization.

The giant 18-pound peacock bass was taken from a lagoon tributary called Trimph which lies about 4 hours north of the village of Sao Felix. The two anglers caught three over 15 pounds and 14 others over 10 that July day. The big fish were all taken on Rat-L-Traps fished in slow moving water. Peacocks up to 15 pounds have also been taken from the Chada area, according to Clement.

The best bait for the moving water of the Xingu is normally a Rat-L-Trap or Brute Sugar Shad. Peacocks hang out around the boulders and rocks blocking the swift water, in the small lagoons off the river, and in front of the small, tributary creeks. They also hide behind islands and off sandbars in small inlets where the currents are not heavy.

Multi-Specie Strikes

Most anglers catch a variety of fish when visiting the Xingu. On many days, two guys can catch 40 or 50 of five or six species. Seldom, if ever, will an angler be skunked. Something is always biting here.

On my trip to the Xingu, I caught a variety of fish each day, but I had help. After a very slow first day, Clement brought along the village witch to cast a spell on the fish. That seemed to work and the fishing improved on days two and three. Overall, I caught several golden peacock of about 8 pounds, at least two dozen crocodile perch up to 17 pounds and payara and bicuda to around 30 inches long. Big piranha were very abundant.

The world's largest red breast piranha swim in the Rio Xingu. (photo by David Orndorf)

There are two types of the dagger-toothed payara in the Xingu. The larger ones run mostly between 10 and 15 pounds, but larger ones have been caught. In fact, Clement believes that someday someone will catch a record-breaking payara there. The other cachorra, a smaller type of payara with finer teeth and some red on its tail, only grows to around 5 pounds. The water is higher in May and early June, and it is usually then when the payara stack up in the rapids.

The Xingu offers bicuda to about 40 inches and piranha to almost 9 pounds. The bicuda is a long, narrow fish with a pointed, "beak-like" snout. One that is 36 inches long may only weigh 5 to 8 pounds. The red-brested piranha grow to about 9 pounds in the dark waters.

There are also monster catfish and two or three other sportfish species that grow to 10 pounds or so in the Xingu. Normally, the many varieties of catfish are caught at night. Redtail catfish grow to a little over 100 pounds and the jau grow to over 200 pounds. The largest one, called a fillot, commonly grows to over 200 pounds, and Clement has heard of catches weighing more than 700 pounds.

"Our cook Sonya, has told me that when she was young, her brother and her were in a dugout canoe when they hooked a fillot on a hand line," says Clement. "The fish dragged the canoe all over the river all day long. Then, they finally got it up alongside of the canoe and killed it with a machete. When they pulled it into the canoe, the canoe sank."

The Xingu, with its fast water, midstream boulders, rocky islands, and deep pools, offers excellent fishing for a variety of species, such as giant bicuda.

Frontier Settlement Selection

Sao Felix du Xingu is the frontier "town" where the lodge is located in the southern part of Para. Up river by boat from Sao Felix du Xingu on the north side is Indian territory. The south side is open for settlement, according to Clement who established his fishing operation on the river after much exploration.

For many years Clement traveled to the typical Brazilian tourist centers such as Rio de Janeiro and Cabo Frio. He still had an interest, though, in going deep into the jungle - where few normally venture.

"About 14 years ago, I asked the travel agent in Brasilia to send me some place where nobody goes," says Clement. "I spent four days on the Aruguaia near the Ile do Bananal, two days in Tucuma and three days on the beautiful Xingu. I fell in love with the Xingu and started to come back every few months. The more I came back, the more people I met and I started putting down roots."

"About 10 years ago I quit my job as a stockbroker in the United States, and I came down here with the idea of setting up a fishing camp," he continues. "I originally opened the Xingu Lodge as a restaurant, but now it is our base of operations. Now I'm having the time of my life taking people who enjoy South America up the river to see the forests and the monkeys in the trees and, of course, catch some fish."

"The Land Where No One Walks"

Sao Felix is quite isolated. In fact, their telephone system was installed just a couple of years ago. Flights in and out by small commuter planes have only become regular in the past four years. There are about

Some of Brazil's most primitive Indians dwell along the main trunk of the Xingu, including the Kaipo Nation's Kuben-Kra. They live in an area called the "Land Where No One Walks."

eight thousand people living in the town of dirt streets and intermittent electrical power, but there's still a lot of exploring to do along the Xingu.

Some of Brazil's most primitive Indians dwell along the main trunk of this bluewater river. The major group are the Kaipo Nation, which is made up of several "aldea" or subgroups. In the Xingu region are the Goia Tire who live near Tucuma, the Cirnkatun, the Koriemora, and the Kuben-Kra. The latter live about 6 hours upstream from Sao Felix in the area Indigina Gaia Tierre which is also called the "Land Where No One Walks." That part of the Xingu is fortunately difficult to access through big rapids and is off-limits to most visitors.

"The Indians there are very primitive," says Clement. "They remain isolated and out of contact. They are the ones that everyone has seen in National Geographic with the paint and feathers."

"I've been to their festivals and danced with them all night long," notes the operator. "They are really a lot of fun but it can get a little wild. They do have firearms and shoot them into the air periodically in the night, as they dance. If you've got a weak heart, it's probably not good."

A Blastin' Good Time

The Indians on the Xingu use guns, bow and arrow and a very heavy club but not the blowguns that are employed by their counterparts in some areas of the Amazon. One of their most interesting festivals is the Festival of the Jubita which involves a large land turtle. The Indians go into the jungle and collect several turtles which they put live on long poles in a rack fashion.

"When they have maybe 100 to 150 of them, they'll build a big fire in the compound," says Clement. "Then, they let the coals die down and put these racks of jubita in the coals. They cover them with banana leaves and let them slow cook. Then, everyone gets in there with their hands and opens them up and eats them."

The Indians practice a little agriculture, primarily planting manioca or corn. They also do a lot of fishing and hunting and they "make trouble", as they did for a couple of Americanos who ventured too far into their area. There are very few netters along the river, but there is some commercial fishing via hand lines for the town market.

I had the unnerving experience of meeting the chief and eight of his followers when they stopped in one night to see Clement on their way to an Indian nation tribal meeting further downriver. Sporting body war paint and long sticks through their lower lip, they surrounded Clement and I as we sat at a candle-lit table in his lodge (the town's power was out). The Indians were friendly on this interaction in the relative safety of town, but if we had motored through their restricted territory upstream, things undoubtedly would have been different.

The area is remote, primitive and harsh, but is ideal for explorers up to the challenge. For more information on Xingu Lodge & Tourism, contact Russ Clement in care of SEI Adventure Travel, 967 W. Wall St., Ste. #130B, Grapevine, TX 76051; (800) 228-3006, (817)424-0248 fax. The Xingu area offers very exciting fishing for a variety of big fish, and it is the fishing that will spoil you in this jungle.

Chapter 9

VENEZUELA'S RANCH LAND LAKES

The fish bully's on the ranch are in the flooded forests

My fourth cast into the flooded jungle drew an explosion. A heavyweight fish with the characteristic three black bars streaked into the nearest submerged hang-up and relieved itself of my plug's extra-strength hardware. Still, my partner smiled and said, "they're here."

Three casts later, I pulled a 12 1/2 pounder from the obstructions, and five minutes after that Robbie had a fish pushing 10 pounds in the boat. We had another five or six explosions that missed their mark and a couple of other fish that we just couldn't pull from the entanglements in the small lake. But, we were happy with our discovery - a lake that had seldom been fished for big peacock bass, with an abundance of them!

My visit to Eastern Venezuela wasn't all action and excitment however. My journey to Ciudad Bolivar began with an overnight stay at Falconcrest Lodge, a very comfortable facility just ten minutes from the airport. The following morning, Robbie Cox who was working for Quest at the time, and I were ready to fish ranch waters just 30 minutes or so from the lodge. Host Jack Starr introduced us to our guide at the lake, and we were soon tossing a variety of baits.

We landed six small peacocks from the flooded trees which covered the 150-acre impoundment. We lost one or two six to eight pound fish in the deeper timber adjacent the large dirt dam, but few other big ones were eye-balled that morning. The reservoir was a "fishy-looking" place with plenty of shallows and deep water. A full moon had apparently affected the "numbers" fishing that owner George had told us about.

The next day, Jack, his son Shawn, Robbie and I traveled about four hours by van to Hato Bayona (ranch) in search of additional ranch lake fishing for bigger peacocks. We found it. Juan Rescaniere, owner of the 250,000 acre ranch, welcomed us at his comfortable five-bedroom hacienda perched high on a tall hill overlooking his ranch and several lakes. The panoramic view is inspiring. Juan showed us around, and we had time for a dip in the spring-fed "marichal" or oasis near the large house.

We were shown the ranch's landing strip for small planes and the vast natural resources present on the land. The ranch itself is teaming with wildlife. We noticed several deer, fox, wild hogs, capybarra, alligators, macaws, scarlet ibis, rosette spoonbills, doves, quail and other creatures while motoring through the dry hill country of Hato Bayona. A breeze kept the rooms cool at night, and the fishing in the main lake was hot most of the day.

Robbie and I concentrated on that clear, black-water lake only one day. It was about 50 acres in size, but approximately 80 percent of it was too shallow (less than 3 feet deep) to attract large peacock. The majority of the big grande pavon were in a 200 yard area that encompassed the deep water. The 30-yard wide stretch was also the only water with flooded timber. The dead trees, some up to two feet in diameter, were generally standing or fallen in depths of 8 to 15 feet.

Timber Testimony

In our seven hours of fishing, my partner and I caught 46 peacock and two payara. The bass ranged from 16 under 5 pounds, to 23 between 5 and 10 pounds, up to 3 that were 11 1/2, 12 and 12 1/2 pounds (all were approximately 28 1/2" to 29" length and 18 1/2" girth). High winds and no trolling motor on the leaky, 16-foot aluminum boat limited our ability to position the boat for optimal casting and battling the biggest fish. As a result, we lost several other peacocks that would have exceeded 10 pounds.

Several of our fish were taken by trolling large topwater plugs along the face of the standing timber. One huge laydown that jutted out into our "trolling" area offered an obstacle that we were soon cussing. Several 10 pound plus fish used the limbs on that deadfall to escape our hook-up. One or two fish broke off in the tree and 3 or 4 others hung our plug on one of its substantial limbs and pried itself loose of the trebles.

We stuck to large baits, such as the Big Game Woodchopper and Magnum Jerkin' Sam, in order to determine the maximum size of peacock available in the spring-fed lake. Robbie and I were checking out

*T*he flooded timber in the small stock tank yielded peacocks up to 10 pounds. The larger ranch lake with deeper water produced the big peacocks.

the waters for future offerings to Quest's clientele. The fish were definitely abundant in that one area of the lake and we could have caught even more that day by throwing smaller plugs and from an electric-motor equipped boat.

Prime Lunker Habitat

On the following day after checking out two more lakes, we slipped back into the main lake and chunked some more giant baits. A 14 1/2 pounder smashed my clown-pattern Woodchopper as our boat was pinned against a fence row (complete with barbed wire), but I worked it out of three submerged brush piles/fallen trees to the boat. Robbie used my fish grabbers to lip the fish at boatside.

We weighed the fish on my certified scales, measured it (30" length, 20" girth) and took a few photos of the trip's largest peacock before releasing it. In the following two hours we caught a couple more 10 pound plus fish and lost another five to the timber or, in one case, a weak split ring on the giant topwater plug.

The main lake has an abundance of forage and the tannin-stained waters that grande pavon prefer and prosper in. A second, much smaller lake was full of flooded timber, baitfish and similar water, but most of it was less than 3 feet deep. Some fishable deep water existed however, and Robbie and I caught 7 or 8 peacock up to about 5 pounds from it one

The clown-pattern Big Game Woodchopper fooled several big peacock in the small lake at Hato Bayona. The author's 14 1/2 pounder was the biggest of the peacocks pulled from the submerged trees.

morning. We lost a couple larger and saw one that probably would have went 8 pounds or so.

Five of the smaller peacocks came from the base of a massive tree surrounded by 4 1/2 feet of water. That was enough encouragement to see the potential in the small 6-acre pond, and to let 15-year old Shawn have a shot at a "birthday" bass before the sun set. The youngster's birthday was actually the day before, but his efforts to catch a peacock in the main lake were to no avail.

Birthday Bass

"Robbie, why don't we take Shawn over to that big tree where the peacocks still may be concentrated?" I asked my partner.

"We'll have him toss a small topwater bait to the area and he can catch his birthday bass," I continued. Robbie agreed that the spot held the highest potential and the sun was going down fast. We quickly paddled to the tree and positioned the boat about 30 feet away.

"Now toss this plug about 10 feet to the right of that big tree," I coached, as Robbie and I watched. Shawn's cast went astray and landed about 10 feet to the left of the tree.

"Oh no, bring it back in quickly and re-cast...to the right," I advised.

A couple of guides show off the skins of male and female boa constrictors killed a few weeks before in the local swimming hole. We cooled off in the tiny spring run without incident

Shawn started reeling the small topwater directly to the boat, but the plug only made it about 15 feet before an explosion stopped its progression. The big peacock charged back to the surface and leaped about 3 feet into the air with the plug rattling against its gill cover. Two more jumps and the fish was tiring. Steady pressure led it to the boat and Robbie's sure grip-lock.

"My birthday bass," smiled Shawn as my partner held up the big peacock for the youngster to admire. We weighed the 9 1/2 pound peacock on my certified scales and released what could have been that small pond's biggest fish. I flew out of San Tome back to Caracas and the United States with memories of Shawn's "birthday" bass on my mind. What a set-up!

Time-Limited Action

Today, Quest offers this lake and a variety of other small water fishing opportunities on private ranches in Venezuela known collectively as Peacock Star Camps. They are ideal for anglers seeking lots of action in a limited amount of time, according to outfitter Scott Swanson.

"The lakes receive little sportfishing pressure and are not dramatically affected by fluctuating water levels as are most river systems," he says. "The lakes, which vary in size and habitat available to fish, are rotated to minimize pressure. Most have standing timber and vegetation banks while a few have rocky shoals and numerous points."

Most of the lakes are easily accessible to comfortable lodging and near commercial air transportation. For more information on the ranch "honey hole" Hato Bayona, or the other 3-day fishing opportunities in

Shawn Starr (l) and Robbie Cox (r) admire the 15-year-old's largest peacock. His "birthday bass" weighed 9 1/2 pounds and struck the topwater bait "on command."

eastern Venezuela, contact Scott Swanson at Quest, 3595 Canton Hwy., Ste. C-11, Marrietta, GA 30066 or phone (888) 891-3474.

Chapter 10

WORLDLY LOCATIONS FOR ACTION

Spanning the globe for some additional highs

Many locations in the world provide peacock bass anglers with all the action they can handle. Addicts are "born" with a minimum of exposure to the peacock bass. Anglers in South Florida, Hawaii, and other spots in South America obsess on the fish. Despite all my travels over the years, I haven't experienced all the locations nor all the outfitters who offer such hook-ups.

There are several additional trips that I intend to make to check out new frontiers, so my work is cut out for me. It seems that new outfitters, operators and agents are growing at times, more rapidly than even the sport. While I continue to discover what's out there for us addicts, there are some additional existing and upcoming opportunities that should be highlighted. Let's take a look at some of them.

Florida Peacocks Up Close

The butterfly peacock bass are doing well in South Florida, as I found out on a recent trip with Fisheries Research Biologist Paul Shafland and peacock-specialist guide Alan Zaremba. We caught several peacocks and largemouth in the small lakes and canals near Miami. Zaremba has a full-size bass boat that he launches even on some of the tiny, dirt "ramps" that cut into the canal banks.

We didn't land any of the larger butterflies that swim in those waters but we did find fish of about 3 pounds. The largemouth seem to thrive side-by-side with the peacocks. Our small topwater baits seemed to produce better on that day than did the other Zaremba favorite, a plastic jerkbait. When you can't or won't leave the continental United States for

G uide Alan Zaremba shows off a couple of typical Florida peacock bass. The butterfly peacock species grow to just over 10 pounds. Fishing here can be very productive with 20 to 30 fish catches, according to the guide. Five and six pounders are taken on occasion also, and numerous peacock around four pounds can be found on one of the better days. Zaremba normally fishes his peacock parties all day, and some of the by-catch may include largemouth, snook, tarpon and large panfish.

a chance at one of the truly giant peacock (speckled or grande), then this fishery is an easy choice.

I highly recommend Zaremba, because on a daily basis, the full-time peacock guide is intimately familiar with the launch areas and the most productive canals in the thousand miles plus of water in Broward and Dade Counties. He can be reached at 1604 N. Park Rd., Hollywood, FL 33021 or phone him at (954)961-0877 to set up a trip.

Fishing the Florida canals without a guide is easier for those who obtain copies of the "angler friendly" canal fishing maps now available from the Florida Game and Fresh Water Fish Commission (GFC) Free copies are available by writing the GFC Fisheries Research Lab, 801 N. W. 40th St., Boca Raton, FL. 33431, according to Shafland, lab director. Copies are also available at participating bait and tackle stores in the Broward/Dade area.

Brochures are available on the following Dade County Canals: Tamiami Canal (C-4), Snake Creek Canal (C-9), Cutler Drain Canal (C-100), Black Creek Canal (C-1), and Snapper Creek Canal (C-2). Cypress Creek Canal (C-14) in Broward County is also available as well as another brochure focusing on boat ramps accessing canals popular with butterfly peacock fishermen. Each angler guide includes a full-page map showing locations of roads, flood control structures, significant landmarks, and directions from the Florida Turnpike or I-95.

"The narrative of each guide provides the angler with an overview of the fish present in the canal, the relevant fishing regulations, and brief descriptions of exotic fish not encountered elsewhere in Florida," Shafland said. "The angler guides are sort of like one-stop shopping for the south Florida angler interested in tapping the sport fishery which exists in the extensive canal system. The narrative tells the reader when, where and how to catch each species present."

Hawaii's Hula Peacock

My wife, Lilliam, and I met guide John Jardin on a trip to Kauai in late 1997. It was my third trip to the islands and I had done the beach and volcano things, so I had to chase after a few peacock bass. Jardin, winner of the Bassin' Big Bass World Championship a few years ago, has been catching peacock bass in Hawaiian waters for over 15 years.

We started off fishing for peacock and largemouth in Kauai's Waita Reservoir. That's where the guide's biggest largemouth was taken. It weighed eight and one quarter pounds. We didn't catch any lunkers that morning, but we did catch maybe a dozen peacock and largemouth up to about 3 pounds. It was an active and very enjoyable half day trip to waters that saw no other anglers that day.

The expert angler's biggest peacock weighed 7 1/2 pounds and was caught on a topwater popper at a small reservoir near Halfway Bridge, called "Number 39". The state record peacock weighed 9 pounds, 4 ounces and was caught in the same reservoir.

"Some of the 30 to 35 Kauai reservoirs have names and others have only numbers," explains Jardin. "All of them are private, except for one in Kokia which is a trout fishery. About 75 percent of the reservoirs on Kauai have both peacock and largemouth bass."

"Waita Reservoir is typically stained because it's so shallow and the wind is always blowing," says the guide. "It might turn a little bit clearer when we have a week or two without wind. The deepest spot is around 12 or 18 feet depending on water level."

Some clearer and deeper reservoirs offer even better peacock bass fishing. They're a lot more inaccessible since they are located further into the cane fields or coffee fields and are mostly gated off.

"It seems like there are more peacocks now than ever before," says Jardin. "Back when we first started to fish in the reservoirs, there weren't that many; we caught more largemouth."

Peacock bass were introduced in the late 1950's. The best months for catching peacock bass are in July and August. Peacocks bed in June

Guide John Jardin knows where the peacock on Kauai, Hawaii are holding up. We took several up to about 3 pounds on a beautiful reservoir one morning. Jardin offers half-day or full-day trips for one person at $100 and $170, respectively. A two-people guide trip would be $170 for a half day and $280 for all day. Jardin's typical clients are bass fishermen from the states who fish on the weekend. They've heard a lot about the peacock bass and want to catch them while they're in Hawaii doing things other than fishing.

and July and then swim around with their fry for about two months, according to Jardin.

"The best lures for peacocks on Kauai are surface plugs and shallow running jerkbaits," he says. "Crankbaits sometimes are effective when fished pretty fast. Peacock are typically caught in water anywhere from 0 to 3 feet. When fishing live bait, we find them deeper on structure, rocks, stumps or tree branches."

"Rain can affect peacock bass if a big rise in the water level occurs and the water turns dirty," explains Jardin. "The fish become scattered and fishing is tough. The rainy season starts around February and ends after April. That's when the water may come up fast. The fishing then is up and down at that time."

Waita varies from 450 acres to about 640 acres when full. There are two creeks or irrigation canals that connect with Waita, and sometimes the fish feed along them when the water's moving, or when the water level is higher. The fishable portion extends 700 yards or so and offers some rocks and a few fence lines.

"Once the water gets up," says Jardin, "there are weeds hanging over the water called buffalo grass. They're not aquatic weeds, but the matted type of grass will grow in water and hold peacock bass. It grows like a bamboo but kind of crawls on the ground."

The summer and winter months are Jardin's busiest time of the year. Jardin's guide service fishes Waita and Aepo Reservoirs. His biggest peacock from the latter, which covers only about 80 acres, weighed five and a half pounds. For more information on this interesting fishery, contact John Jardin, at JJ's Big Bass Tours, P.O. Box 248, Kalaheo, HI 96741; or phone (808) 332-9219.

Lago Balbina and Rio Tupana

I revisited Balbina Reservoir north of Manaus, Brazil recently with friend and avid fisherman Marco Lima and found plenty of small peacock action there. Many of our 20 fish over a four hour expedition were between 3/4 and 2 pounds, but I did catch one that was 8 1/2 pounds. The fish caught and released in the timbered impoundment included several with blue fins, many with irregular black splotches on their sides and schools of small butterfly peacocks.

New restrictions in 1999 will make commercial fishing on Balbina Reservoir illegal. While fishing the lake in late 1998, I noted the presence of freshwater porpoise or "boto", as they are called in Brazil. There appears to be plenty of forage for them in Balbina.

Lima and his wife, Nete, operate a very comfortable lodge on the Tupana River, a tributary of Brazil's Rio Madeira. The Tupana area has several lakes and small resacas which offer numerous guarapes or creeks, laydowns, bars and rock outcroppings which attract big peacock bass.

It also offers a variety of bird and animal life to view. In fact, it was here that I saw my first and only jaguar in the wild, after 40 trips to the rainforest. The big cat was swimming across the river in front of us as we motored upstream. We boated within 30 feet of the wet jaguar and watched it climb the river bank and quickly disappear into the jungle, an impressive sight!

Lodge visitors take a 35 minute commercial flight from Manaus to Borba and then travel about an hour and 45 minutes by comfortable, covered speed boat to the lodge. Fishing is from 18 foot aluminum skiffs with small outboards and electric trolling motors.

"Good anglers can expect to catch 15 to 30 peacocks per day," notes Marco Lima. "Most will be above 4 pounds and some will weigh as much as 15 to 20 pounds. We have over 500 miles of fishing spots and have even caught payara up to 26 pounds. We operate in the late summer and early fall months when water levels here are ideal."

The lodge is constructed on two floating platforms, a two-story sleeping quarters and a very nice lounge/dining room pavilion. The 9 spacious rooms have air conditioning, screened veranda and private baths. The lounge/dining pavilion, built of natural wood materials, includes a bar, lobby and large surrounding sun deck.

Jaguar are a rare sighting during daylight hours, but at night, they roam the rain forest. My Tupana sighting was a first for me.

For information on this operation, contact Marco Lima, Tupana Fishing Lodge, Conjunto Eldorado Bloco 31 APTO 23B Chapada, Manaus Amazonas Brazil. CEP 69050-000; phone 011-55-92-642-5733 (after 5 p.m.) or 011-55-92-642-6721. In the U.S. call (800)780-4AIR.

Other Brazilian Discoveries

Friend Len Zolna of Spring Lake Park, Minnesota reported an excellent trip on the Discovery, a floating hotel owned by Brazilian Kadu Berni. Berni is a writer, film maker and expert fisherman who decided to become an outfitter recently. On his recent trip to the Rio Negro with Berni, Zolna called the "Peacock Bass Explosions" T-Shirts they all wore their "secret weapons."

"Your advice to go for doubles worked great for my brother and me," he told me. "We caught more doubles than anyone else. Our best lures were the Woodchoppers and the 3/4 ounce Krocodile hammered bronze with orange strip spoons. On one day, we caught 51 peacocks."

I haven't been on this trip yet, but reports are that the boat is first class. Contact Tim Anderson at Jungle's Edge Tours, c/o Menna Travel, 4111 Central Ave. N. E. St. 107, Minneapolis, MN 55421; or phone (800)635-2032 for more information on this trip.

Venezuela's Pasimoni Activity

The Pasimoni and Pasiba rivers watersheds in southern Venezuela offer fishing for "grande" peacocks. You will not catch big numbers of pavon here, but the size can be impressive. Several IGFA and NFWF line class records were set here in the early 90's, including several of mine.

High water levels affect the fishing drastically on this waterway, and several years have offered only a handful of "fishable" weeks. Trip

Jack Wadkins, of Naples, Florida fished Peru with Amazonia Expeditions, and while the peacock fishing was slow, he was able to catch by far the largest aruana that I have ever seen. The world mark is approximately 13 pounds, and he reportedly caught a 40 pounder. I have caught and seen photos of some between 8 and 10 pounds, but his monster caught from the Tahuayo River on a green Artic Spinner was extraordinary. It jumped 30 times and became entangled briefly in an underwater snag before he landed it.

cancellations for high waters are common and very justifiable. A good agent will always cancel such trips rather than allow his customers to go ahead and experience lousy fishing. The Amazonas Peacock Bass Safari Camp is very rustic and the logistics are time-consuming. The 11 day trip package allows only 6 days of fishing. Anglers fish from 16-foot aluminum boats, and the available Indian guides have fished and boated the area for years.

This is the water where my partner and I caught and released a 39 pound "double". My 20 pounder was, and still is, a NFWF line class record. Frequent South America angler, Len Kouba, reportedly caught a 16 and a 19 3/4 pounder on the same huge topwater plug, and Bert Bookout caught his 25 pound all-fly tackle record there. But the Pasimoni is moody due to fluctuating water levels. See my "Peacock Bass Explosions" book for more information on this fishery.

Lake Guri Hangs On

Lake Guri, located in eastern Venezuela at the edge of La Gran Sabana, is 90 miles long and 25 miles wide offering hundreds of miles of shoreline, islands, and coves. Fishing however may be spotty. I recently fished the huge, timber-flooded bays near the Caroni River and caught several pretty peacocks that were vivid emerald green with orange accents. Guri offers plenty of grande, butterfly, and royal pavon (Cichla intermedia).

Howler monkeys flourish in the jungle surrounding the lake, and their frequent roaring calls make for an interesting backdrop to the fishing. At times, you can see a group of them jumping from one tree to another.

I stayed at the Paovon Lodge, the name of which comes from the word combination of the nearby town El Pao and the peacock called pavon in Spanish. Four colonial style duplex cabanas offer large and tastefully decorated rooms with private baths, air conditioning, giant porches and hot water. Two "churuatas" or Indian pavilions are the dining quarters and bar. The comfortable accommodations and the level of service make this an excellent choice when fishing Guri. Owner Eduardo Pantoja, who is well known for his excellent Los Roques bonefish operation, has several 16 foot boats powered by 60 hp outboards and trolling motors at Paovon.

Lake Guri fishing can be hot and cold, very cold. Extreme drought here can affect the fishing. While there are a few teeners in Guri, most will be smaller and on some trips, very small fish are the norm for those catching any "numbers" of peacock bass. From the Puerto Ordaz airport, it is a 2 1/2 hour drive through the hilly grasslands to the lake.

El Pao, another operation that lies near the shores of Lake Guri, fishes the sunken forest. Peacock Bay Lodge also is an operation on Lake Guri that offers comfortable accommodations with hot showers and private baths. Fishing is from 18- to 21-foot fiberglass and aluminum boats equipped with 40 h.p. outboards and electric trolling motors.

Just down the road from the Guri operations lies Uraima Camp which is possibly the world's best spot for huge payara. Unfortunately, the boats used in this operation are usually 45 to 60-foot long dugouts which are cumbersome, difficult to maneuver and control in the rapids... which is where the fish hang out. See my "Peacock Bass & Other Fierce Exotics" book for detailed information on this area and many others around the world offering exciting, addictive angling.

Chapter 11

TUCURUI AND OTHER NORTHEAST BRAZIL HOTSPOTS

The many productive peacock waters in the State of Para

It was the final day of the tournament. Dick Ballard and I were trolling mid-day to cool off and, frankly, because strikes in our key casting spots had slowed. We had a good catch but needed another couple of big fish to take the prize.

Puttering along in a trolling pass by a brushy point, the boat veered slightly to the left to bounce off an obstruction. I felt a jolt as my rod tip bucked towards the surface. A peacock of 10 or 11 pounds blew up the surface going skyward, as the boat slowed, out of gear. Our boat's momentum forced the peacock again to jump out of the water in an irate mood.

Then after a third jump trying to throw the big spoon, it dove into a large tree snag. My 40-pound test monofilament separated, and my hopes were dimmed. Submerged brush and trees in Lago de Tucurui make landing the big fish of the day difficult, and a fish of that size is a giant currently in this impoundment.

Tucurui, which is an indian word meaning "River of Ants", is massive; the power-generating reservoir in the Brazilian state of Para stretches about 220 miles to the fourth largest hydroelectric dam in the world. While the upper end of Tucurui offers rapids, rocky stretches and payara or "cachorra", most of the 1,555 square mile reservoir in the lower end contains flooded forests with big peacock bass.

The peacocks in the Tucurui region of the Amazonas take an assortment of lures. These aggressive fish grow to over 15 pounds in the reservoir.

The reservoir has had its share of logging, although the reservoir's fertile bottom with millions of trees still emerging is located in the middle of the rain forest. Many of the largest trees however, have been sawed off right at the water line. They pose a danger to the boater.

One of the local loggers even developed an underwater chain saw which can cut the trunks four to six feet below the surface. Unfortunately, the lake level fluctuates 10 to 12 feet. If they cut the trees while the water level is near its peak, the sawn-off stumps will be at a dangerous place when the lake drops.

Tournament Time

Ballard and I finished the "no-release" event in seventh place with 26 1/2 pounds of tucunare. We caught many of our fish in an area we called "Laydown Cove". It yielded 22 pounds of peacock that day including my 7 pounder. Most of our strikes were on big Luhr-Jensen #18 Pet Spoons, many while being trolled.

The Amazon Sport Fishing Tournament held on Lake Tucurui in September of 1996 was the organizers' initial attempt to put together a national or international peacock bass event. Headquarters was the town of Tucurui located at the dam, and the Tocantins River below it. Tournament Director Elza Queiroz did a tremendous job putting the event together with help from Chris Serrao of Paratur and many others.

Rodrigo Lopez and his son, who live on the lake, won the tournament prize: a boat and motor. Their tally was 32 peacock bass that weighed 128 pounds. Second place went to two other local guys that amassed 68 small peacocks weighing 125 pounds. Big fish of the event was an 11 pounder taken by Bruno Parreira of Sao Paulo. He won a boat, motor and trailer.

Several Brazilian TV networks covered the event and the practice round. In fact, Global Network, the largest national network in South America, aired taped interviews with me and a catch-and-release segment of one of my fish. It's probable that it was the first time "release" had ever been shown on Brazilian TV. Such a "concept" was unfortunately "foreign" to many of the peoples of that country which eat most everything caught.

Stressing Catch-And-Release

Asked for comments about the event, I stressed catch-and-release requirements, numerous rule changes and other ideas which are common in U.S. tournaments but foreign there. I suggested a minimum length and quantity limits for the event, in addition to the catch and release.

The second annual tournament in August of 1997 was happily focused more on conservation. Numerous rule changes occurred in the second annual event. Queiroz changed the first year's totally unlimited and unrestricted creel to a six peacock per day - minimum length of 16 inches per two-man team for this event.

The waters of Lake Tucurui were unusually high and the fish were deep, but there were a good number of peacock bass between 6 and 10 pounds taken. The most productive method in the second event was trolling large diving plugs and spoons over vast stretches of the reservoir arm. Antonio Lopes, trolling a spoon, caught the largest peacock which weighed 12 pounds, 12 ounces. Helder Furman and Mauricio da Costa were the winning team, catching a total of 12 peacock bass that weighed 57 pounds, 3 ounces.

The tournament was sponsored by the State Government of Para, Paratur, Exatur, the town of Tucurui, Eletronorte, Radio & TV Floresta, Unigraf, Skol, ACIT, and others. Most contestants stayed at the comfortable Lake Tucurui Hotel. Food in their very nice restaurant is excellent. For information on the event, contact Elza Queiroz at Exatur, Centro Comercial, B1-R - Loja 03, CEP 68464-000 Vila Permanente, Tucurui, Para, Brazil or fax 011-55-91-787-1641.

Pristine Para State

The state of Para has several pristine, fish-laden reservoirs, such as Tucurui, as well as large rivers, natural lakes and streams. The Tapajos, Xingu and Tocantins are very significant tributaries to the mighty Amazon River. The "corridors" of this watershed include the Southeast Araguaia/Tocantins Region, the Central Amazon Lakes Region, the Western Tapajos/Trombetas Region and the South Central Xingu Region, which is covered in the previous chapter.

*L*ago de Tucurui has plenty of cover in some areas of the impoundment.
In others, loggers have eliminated much of it.

In the waters of Para, you can catch seven different species of freshwater sportfish that each grow to over 15 pounds (7 kilos). You can battle giant peacock bass (tucunare) to 25 pounds, cachorra (payara) to 30 pounds, crocodile perch (trairao) to 25 pounds, striped catfish (suribim pintado) to 80 pounds, pacu to 20 pounds, tambaqui to 20 pounds and cachara to 20 pounds. Several more species, such as bicuda, matrinxa, aruana, corvina (pescada do piaui), curimbata, piranha (red, black and silver species) and apapa (sardinata), grow to 10 or more pounds. Four additional species of monster catfish (jau, piraracu, piraiba and dorada) grow to over 100 pounds.

Tucurui & Tributaries

The giant Lake Tucurui, formed by the damming of the Rio Tocantins/Araguaia, lies in the southeast region of the state. The primary tributaries of the Araguaia are the Campo Alegre, Iraja, Arraias Jo Araguaia, Agua Fria, Itacaiunas. The Araguaia flows north from its headwaters in the state of Mato Grosso approximately 930 miles through the state of Para into Tucurui at the town of Maraba. The Tocantins River enters the reservoir from the state of Goias to the east and leaves through the Tucurui dam, flowing approximately 400 miles to join up with the Baja de Marajo near Belem.

There are only two major falls on the waterway, and once the locks at Tucurui are complete, you will be able to navigate its entire length. Very few rapids are present in the smaller tributaries. Numerous small lagoons on the upper end, and a few on the lower end, offer peacock bass and small cachorra. Larger catfish are often taken on the upper end of the tributary, as well as the unique 5-barred peacock bass.

*P*eacock bass in the lakes off the Rio Trombetas will often go berserk and try to destroy huge topwater plugs. The author caught and released several like this 17 1/2 pounder on a couple of trips to these waters.

At the southern-most point of the state of Para between the east and west branches of the Araguaia lies the world's largest river island, Bananal. The optimal fishing conditions for chasing peacock bass in the northern area of this southeast region are September to December, and in the southern area, from April to October. At Lake Tucurui, March to December are considered the best months to fish peacocks.

Central Amazon Lakes Region

The Amazon River is deep and wide here, and this corridor is a massive collection point of enriched waters from its large tributaries, the Trombetas, Tapajos, Xingu and Jari. The Amazon River area spans 2,600 miles through the state of Para, and numerous large, natural lakes and lagoons offer good fishing for trophy peacock bass, giant catfish and piraracu. Most of the blackwater lakes are linked to the Amazon via dead-water channels, and many are interconnected by canals (paranas).

Lago Grande near Santarem is over 60 miles long and 30 miles wide and just one of the many adjacent to the Amazon River. A huge lake at the juncture of the Xingu and Amazon is almost 150 miles long and up to 15 miles wide. Knowledgeable, fishermen live along the corridor and know where to find the big ones. In general, the optimal fishing conditions are from September to December during the low water times.

Tapajos/Trombetas Tributes

The area's fishing is diverse from the predominant giant peacock bass waters of the Trombetas and Nhamunda rivers and adjacent lakes in the northern portion to the more diverse and faster-water fishing of the Tapajos and its tributaries on the southern side of the region.

Two huge tributaries, the 1200 mile long Teles Pires and the 1100 mile long Juruena, form the Tapajos which drains north another 930 miles to the Amazon at Santarem. At least 7 major rapids exist on the Tapajos and 10 others are found along the Teles Pires. The Jamanxim, a major, 750-mile-long tributary, flows parallel to the Tapajos, and like most other tributaries is replete with rapids. The upper end of the Tapajos contains many small, fishy lagoons, but most of its stream bed lies in deep valleys surrounded by the Brazilian Highlands. Other important tributaries of the north-flowing Tapajos include the Crepori, Arapiuns, Sao Benedito, Cristalino, Tropas, Cururu-ri and Preto Cururu Acu. Most offer brightly-colored peacock bass and a dozen or more additional trophy-sized gamefish like payara (cachorra), bicuda, matrinxa, trieda (trairao), piranha and suribim pintado.

From the Guyana Highlands, the 1,000-mile-long Trombetas flows south through the rainforest to link up with the Amazon near Santarem. The upper end of the blackwater river contains major rapids as it courses through the mountains. The lower end is deep and wide and a major transportation route for ore tankers. Along the lower end to the rapids at Acampamento are numerous natural lakes loaded with giant peacock bass and hungry piranha. Near Port Trombetas, Lake Erepucu is almost 60 miles long and contains large peacocks. So does nearby Lake Abui.

The fairly inaccessible Jari River offers good fishing for big peacock bass in a steep-banked stream above the rapids and waterfalls. Like other south-flowing rivers in the area, there are plenty of rock gardens and boulders and just a few swampy areas. The Paru River, located 60 miles west of the Jari, also offers good fishing above the rapids. The rapids, in general, protect the peacock bass and other sport fish from the porpoises.

To the west, the lagoons and lakes off the Nhamunda River offer excellent fishing. Other forest-covered tributaries north of the Amazon include the Mapuera, Erepecuru (Paru de Oeste), Cachorra, Maicuru and Curuapanema. Most of them also contain numerous rapids, big sandbars and deep-water pools with peacock bass and cachorra.

Optimal peacock fishing conditions for the north & central areas are from September to December and for the southern areas are March to October. For additional information on many of these areas, see chapter 6 in "Peacock Bass Explosions" and chapter 7 in "Peacock Bass & Other Fierce Exotics".

Chapter 12

MATO GROSSO GOLD

Chasing the elusive golden dorado in the Great Swamp

Phil Jensen set back hard on the rod and the golden dorado shot into the air. It was our first glimpse of the famous, stunning yellow "dourado", as it is called in the Pantanal area. The small six-pounder displayed its ferocity by jumping all over the small tributary as Phil tried to put its brakes on. Finally, he got the fish under control, and our guide netted it.

We slowly motored upstream in the narrow waterway trolling minnow baits about 60 feet behind the boat. It was my turn. Another dorado of about the same size slammed my lure and became aerial. Three leaps later, it had tossed my lure back toward the boat. "So Foy"; it was gone.

I was able to land a smaller dorado later in the day, but the fishing for them was slow for those using artificials in the Paraguay River tributaries that April. Phil, President of Luhr-Jensen Lures, and I had taken a couple of extra days after the annual FEIPESCA tackle trade show in Sao Paulo to fly into Corumba in southwestern Brazil for a taste of the Pantanal wetlands fishing. Corumba, a major port city for soy and ore shipments, lies across the Rio Paraguay from Bolivia.

At Corumba, we met Paulo Cora who transferred us to the Hotel Porto Morrinho, a very modern and comfortable facility in the South Pantanal. Cora is owner/manager of Hotel Porto Morrinho conveniently located on the banks of the Rio Paraguay. The river which stretches 1550 miles, acts as the border between Bolivia and Paraguay.

From the charming hotel, anglers can venture to the Miranda, Taquari and Abobral rivers in Brazil, as well as the numerous bays or

Piraputanga are a schooling fish that generally range up to about 5 pounds. While they are normally caught all year long, the best months are when rivers are full, in the summer.

"baias" in the marshy area. The best fishing in the immediate vicinity may be on the Rio Taquari, which lies off the Rio Paraguay upstream from Porta de Manga.

Considered the world's biggest wetland area, the Pantanal covers 57,000 square miles in the upper Paraguay River Basin. The majority of its coverage lies in Brazil in the states of Mato Grosso and Mato Grosso do Sul, but portions extend into Bolivia and Paraguay.

The oldest maps of South America delineated the area as the "Sea of Xaraes" because the early Portuguese explorers actually thought the basin was a permanent inland sea. Just a little over 200 years ago, the first settlers to the region renamed it "Pantanal," which means "Great Swamp" in Portuguese.

The elevation of the Pantanal is only between 260 and 500 feet, but it is surrounded by beautiful, high plateaus from which the river system springs. The state of Mato Grosso includes a mountain climate, crystalline waterfalls, river beaches, and the rich biodiversity of the Pantanal. Its capital, Cuiaba, is the South American geodesic point and principal city in the region with a population of nearly one million.

Portions of the Pantanal are surrounded by a "campo cerrado" or natural savanna with varying amounts of woody vegetation ranging from brushy grasslands to open forest stands. Within the campo cerrado are small elevated hills called "murundus". Along the rivers are "bocas" or those places where the tributaries break their banks and flow into floodplains, offering excellent opportunities for catching all sportfish.

"Brejos" or low swampy areas at the edges of the river, also may harbor some fish.

In other areas of the Pantanal, open savannas called "campo limpo" surround the waterways. Only a few circular "capaos" or small forest islands in the sea of open savanna provide landmarks.

Piraputanga Passions

While our timing for the dorado fishing was off, the piraputanga were very active. We used light tackle to hook a couple of dozen on tiny spinners and spoons retrieved rapidly across the substantial current. Some of the waters in the Paraguay Basin were muddied from recent rains, and our best spot for the piraputanga was an intersection of two small tributaries. The clearest one, with visibilities of maybe 12 inches, was about 80 feet wide while the muddy one draining farm land was half that size. The schools of fish seemed to hang out around the mudline in the clearer water.

The piraputanga averaged about two to four pounds, but we also hooked several piranha, several small payara or cachorra (dogfish) and a couple of catfish by tying up to the weedy bank and casting across the current. Minnow baits fooled the larger fish and a funny, eel-like minnow, called a "tuvira", garnered a few sizable pacu. The round fish seem to resemble a giant piranha, but the pacu's teeth are square like ours rather than pointed. Surubim catfish grow to around 175 pounds and pacu up to 30 in the Paraguay River area.

Golden Gospel

The dorado are one of Brazil's most sought after sportfish. They normally run around 10 to 12 pounds maximum in the Pantanal, but some grow to 40 pounds. In the Brazilian winter months, dorado have been caught in the area weighing as much as 44 pounds. Most trophies are regularly taken then, however, the giants are very rare.

While Phil and I were in the Pantanal area, a few boats did hook some 10 pounders on natural bait near where we were fishing. Many of the big dorado are taken right from the Paraguay River rocks in front of Parais Du Dorados (Dorado's Paradise) hotel. As the water drops, the current increases and the big fish move into the area.

Cora remembers one giant dorado he caught while playing around with a child's spincast rod and reel outfit. With Mickey Mouse rod in hand, he cast a tiny, one-inch Rapala minnow bait toward the middle of the river. An 8 1/2 pound dorado grabbed the bait and the lure got stuck in its tongue.

April through October is the dry season and June through September are low water times and the best months to catch big golden dorado. Fishing for dorado is often best when the water starts coming down, in July and August. The rainy season is from November through March. Waters are high from January through May, and fish are scattered in the surrounding swamps then, making them difficult to locate.

The most effective artificial lures for dorado are small to medium size, but the smaller ones are prone to be easily destroyed on the initial catch. They will strike larger lures, but the larger hooks are thick and can't penetrate the dorado's mouth as easily. When the dorado jumps, he often will shake his head violently and toss the lure free.

Dorado move about in schools of 20 to 30 fish and feed on baitfish at most levels in the water column, but they don't always strike at a topwater lure. Like many species of schooling fish, all in the same school will normally be the same size.

"The larger dorado have a problem keeping up with the smaller ones because they are not as fast," says Cora. "As a result, they typically move about on or near the bottom in the rivers and streams. You often have to locate them in deep water and catch them there."

Perhaps the best way to locate a dorado is to cover a lot of water by trolling. Crankbaits with lips work well for visiting anglers, but the fish's powerful jaws and sharp teeth can "do a number" on the lures, even those with wooden bodies. As with peacock bass, golden dorado demand strong lures, hooks and terminal tackle. They will easily tear up less. You'll need wire leaders and heavy snap swivels with 20 to 40 pound test monofilament.

Dorado generally are in moving water. If you are casting to the fish, the guide will anchor or tie up to the bank cover near a point or intersection of two creeks. Anglers will cast upstream into riffles and eddies on the far side of the tributary and bring their lures back, across the current. You can also drift downstream and cast, as well as anchor and fish live bait off the points.

In the state of Mato Grosso, one of the best fishing areas for dorado lies in its southern part in the Taquari River, where we fished. The entire river offers excellent fishing, particularly the area near Salorenzo. In Southern Brazil, the best areas for catching big dorado are in the Paraguay and Parana Rivers near the Paraguay border.

Peacock Possibilities

I have it on good authority from more than one source that peacock do exist in the Pantanal and they are spreading. Native to the Amazon,

The author shows off a small, spoon-caught golden dorado from the Pantanal area.

they have been introduced into the massive marsh area along the Bolivian border. So far, they seldom exceed 6 or 7 pounds, but a few isolated areas have big populations of the fish.

From the photos that I have seen, the peacocks there resemble some of those in isolated areas of the Amazon territory with irregular splotches on their sides, several vertical bars and other distinct markings over their entire body.

The future looks bright for the peacock in this region. Sportfishing with artificials is becoming more popular among the primary users of the area - the Brazilians. As a result of the increasing interest, some have stocked land-locked lakes in the region and others have introduced peacocks into Pantanal marsh areas where none previously existed.

In all, the rivers and lakes of the region have a varied fish life that includes over 250 species. There are several species of both piranha and catfish, some of the latter growing as large as 275 pounds.

"July and August are excellent times to catch some of the area's huge catfish," adds Cora. "We catch them on huge, three to four foot long worms. We string the entire length of the worm on a single hook all the way up the line."

"Drifting is a productive technique for catfish or what we call leather fish," he continues. "Pintado can weigh up to about 130 pounds, but we don't see as many as we did a few years ago.

Cora first fished the area in 1986, and claims the dorado fishing is just as good today as it was then. The only thing that is different now is that the catfish are not as large as they were 10 years ago. Anglers caught a lot of big ones then and they took them out, according to the camp manager.

"Now, we see the size of the big ones caught increasing again," he says. "They are getting bigger and bigger."

Water, Water, Everywhere

The "Great Swamp" is not a real swamp at all; it is a floodplain that gets inundated each year during the wet season from December to April. The Pantanal's annual average rainfall of 56 inches flushes through a complex river system and floods about two thirds of the entire area. Since the slope of the Pantanal plain is minimal in the north-south direction, rivers are unable to cope with the rain.

The Pantanal area when full of water in the winter months (our summer months) covers a 10,000 square mile area. The floods inundate all lakes, rivers, streams, and sloughs in the region. The water level is typically highest during month of June and then starts falling.

During the wet season, only islands of forests at higher elevations remain dry. The Pantanal floodplain drains into the Paraguay, South America's second longest river system. The high "flood wave" takes six months to move from the north to the south, and behind it the wetlands slowly return to dry grasslands. In the southern Pantanal, savannas are flooded for a few months after the end of the rainy season.

The lowest water levels in the Pantanal usually occur in December or January, and the rainy season starts to fill the waterways again in February. Water levels increase most in April and May when the differences on the river are very noticeable from one day to the next. It is only after the water recedes that the famous congregations of wildlife build.

Perhaps the most interesting sights in the Pantanal region are the birds. Around 700 species exist in the region, including the very different, giant "tuiuiu" bird. Flocks of them shift around on short trees,

The Pantanal, called the "Great Swamp", offers plenty of water and fish species for anglers. It is also known as the world's biggest ecological sanctuary.

jockeying for the best squatters position. We also noticed the rare and magnificent Jaburu. The giant bird, with a red neck and huge black head, is the biggest stork of the Americas and is known as the symbol of the Pantanal.

The area is an important breeding ground for more common wetland birds such as heron, stork and ibis. Big flocks of each are frequent sightings. There are also some 26 species of parrots including toucans, and the endangered blue hyacinth macaw, which is the world's largest parrot stretching more than three feet long. Although I didn't see one, another bird found in the area is the rhea or Brazilian ostrich. In fact, they are so numerous, that a national park in the state of Mato Grosso do Sul is named after a local population of rheas.

Large ugly birds called nhuma watch the fishing action from shore. Also in abundance around the Pantanal are colhereiros or spoonbills. Several flew over us while fishing. Another group of birds well represented in the area are birds of prey. There are reportedly 45 species of them in the Pantanal ecosystem. Eagles are also fairly abundant.

World's Biggest Ecological Sanctuary

The Pantanal is noteworthy for its abundance of wildlife and is a refuge for many threatened South American mammal species such as jaguar, puma, giant otter, giant anteater, giant armadillo, marsh deer (the largest South American deer), peccary (South America's wild pig), and tapir. The most common animal is the capybara, which is the world's largest rodent weighing up to 150 pounds. During the dry season, massive herds of 100 or more capybara can be seen.

There are five species of monkeys in the region and over 500 species of reptiles. Most evident of the latter are the jacare' or cayman, and the world's largest snake, the anaconda. During my brief visit at a relatively high water time, I noticed several of the jacare' and, fortunately, no snakes.

The flora of the Pantanal is a mixture of woodlands, savanna grasslands, evergreen and semideciduous forest and jungle. Almost all of the Pantanal is privately owned by large cattle ranchers. Over 2,500 "fazendas" offer grasslands to seven million head of cattle. As a result of this use, the region's natural beauty has been left relatively unharmed. IBAMA is the Brazilian Environment Protection Institute and caretaker of their national parks.

World's Largest Tournament

Perhaps the world's largest fishing tournament is held each year on the Rio Paraguay at the town of Caceres. The 3-day event is part of a week-long Festival Internacional de Pesca which offers a variety of activities. The festival and tournament draws thousands of visitors.

In the Pantanal area, there are about 10 significant hotels and 52 large houseboat operations that fish the Paraguay River and surrounding area from Corumba. Most of the boat operations go upriver as far as 120 miles and not down toward Hotel Porto Morrinho. A lot of the boat operations go up to Salorenzo which is toward Quiaba.

For information on this fishery and the Pantanal area, contact Marco Antonio M. Oliveira at Liguepes Brazilian Sport Fishing, Rua Dr. Costa Jr., 390 - Sao Paulo - SP - CEP 05002-000, Brazil or phone (011) 864-0400. For accommodations, contact Jayme Cora, Hotel Porto Morrinho, SuperPesca, Rua da Consolacao, 359-3 And. Conj 31 - Sao Paulo - SP - CEP 01301-000, Brazil or phone (011) 258-4355.

Dorado are definitely the focus in the Pantanal currently, although peacock bass are thriving and slowly expanding their range. Dorado can also be found in Colombia, Argentina, Uruguay and Paraguay. In northern Colombia, they are abundant in Lago de la Raya which is about 400 miles north of Medellin. They grow to 25 pounds there and to about 50 in Paraguay. In Argentina, they grow to around 35 pounds in most waters.

Chapter 13

BATTLES WON AND LOST

Sometimes costly mistakes can't be helped; sometimes they can!

"The net, the net, the net," I shouted at my Portuguese-speaking guide as I pressured the big peacock bass near the boat. Two more short runs peeled line from my heavy casting reel as the drag moaned in discontent, but the battle was almost over. The guide, on his very first day with a client, still had a bewildered look on his face, and, at the time, I didn't know how to say "net" in Portuguese. So, I grabbed the net (or "rede") and handed it to him.

He put the net into the water, and I leaned back on the heavy-action rod to direct the peacock head-first into the net.

"All is well," I thought. "The fish is mine."

But, the guide just froze and didn't lift the net.

"Lift up, lift up," I shouted, realizing he wouldn't understand my English. But I showed him with an upward motion of my forearm, how to accomplish raising the net. He seemed to get the message just before the 12 pound peacock turned and started to swim out of the net.

The fish jerked its head to the side and the lure's trebles popped free just as the guide lifted the net with the peacock inside.

"Whew," I gasped, only to see the big fish wedge its head into a small hole in the net. Then, with a characteristic shake, the peacock tore through it landing back in the water. I watched the fish dive for the depths, as the guide stood looking at the gaping hole in the net.

I shrugged disappointed, shaking my head. Then, I smiled. That fish on a small lagoon off Northern Brazil's Rio Agua Boa had earned its escape. I believe it was destined not to be handled by man that morning. My Ecotur Park Lodge guide had become very sick and my partner and I were dealing with a substitute, with very limited, if any, experience.

All in all, the loss of that fish was no big deal. I have probably caught a hundred larger. But, it reveals that there are many mistakes that can be made throughout the day that will cost you a peacock bass. In South America, it often seems that the ones that do get away are all giants. Big peacock bass certainly have the know-how and the strength to strain the limits of our guides, equipment and our reflexes.

Improper drag setting, for example, is a common fault in the loss of big peacock bass. It is vital to set the drag before the fish strikes, either at home or as conditions change. The drag should be less "giving" in an area of heavy timber and snags than in open water above a sand bar. Some anglers try to adjust the drag while the peacock bass is on. With a giant peacock, even an experienced fisherman can't get away with that.

Catastrophic Cavort

I remember making such a stupid mistake once, and it cost me a 20-pounder. I was fishing a lagoon off the Pasiba River in the Amazonas Territory of southern Venezuela and had caught four peacocks between 18 and 21 pounds already that week. Two were from the same flooded stand of trees that I was again casting toward. I lofted a cast to the edge of the timber and had a monster boil up on it.

I set the hook and held on as the fish swam parallel to the treeline. My drag was clamped down tight and that prevented the 20-plus pounder from moving into the trees. Over the following five minutes, I carefully worked the big peacock away from the entanglements, as my guide thoughtfully paddled our boat toward the center of the cove.

I was about 75 yards away from the potential hang-ups and the fish appeared tired after jumping several times and struggling against my powerful rod. Not wanting the hooks to tear out of the fish at boatside on a last, desperate attempt to escape, I eased back on the star drag ever so slightly. That, I thought, would give me a little safety buffer in case the peacock saw the boat and tried to make another run. The drag then would absorb the shock.

Well, I was right, but I had miscalculated. The giant did indeed see the boat and took off, but it pulled line like I had just hooked a freight train. It headed back for the timber, taking most of my spool of 40 pound test monofilament and smoking my thumb in the process. I tried to stop the fish with the thumb on the revolving spool and got a burn for it.

The fish swam right into the timber, made a right turn and my line separated, sounding like a gunshot. My guide and I sat there in the boat in awe of the fish that we expected to be whipped and safely away from any entanglements. I felt like crying. But, I had only myself to blame.

To land giant peacocks like this one, an angler has to be prepared mentally and equipment-wise. The 20-plus pounders can easily escape an angler or guide who makes mistakes. I have seen novices make many critical mistakes when first seeking trophy peacocks, but with these fish, catastrophic mistakes are easy to make. For those anglers that say, "big peacock bass always seem to get away!", I say get prepared and stay that way. Knowing some of the potential problems to which a giant fighter may be exposed should aid in that preparation.

Unfortunately, anglers are not always prepared mentally to handle a trophy peacock bass when it strikes. Everyone makes mistakes, even the most experienced of us. Poor mental judgment is not inherent only in beginners, but it usually will show up among them more frequently.

I have fished for peacock with more than one hundred anglers, including "name" tournament black bass pros, outdoor TV show hosts, and total novices who had seldom handled a rod and reel. And, I have seen many big peacock bass escape, even from technically-proficient, peacock-experienced fishermen. Yes, I lose some too. Some situations can't be helped, but many can.

Equipment Examinations

Getting a big peacock bass halfway to the boat only to have the hook pull out or the line snap is frustrating. Hopefully, there is something to blame for the loss and a bit of experience to remember. Too, the best anglers will learn from their mistakes.

Having sound equipment and paying proper attention to tackle details really begins prior to the trip. Naturally, sharp hooks are a must. Big hooks which are sometimes more difficult to pull into the hard mouth of a big peacock bass, may fall out easily when they are dull.

Trophy hunters, like me, often fish with big baits expressly for the giants, and equipment should reflect that goal. Large, heavy-duty hooks are thicker than smaller ones and, thus, require sharper points and a more forceful hook set. All factory-made or installed hooks need additional sharpening. I use a hone or file on each lure in my tackle box to get the sharpest point possible. Each morning on the ride out to the fishing grounds, I "touch up" the points on all the baits I will be using that day.

Light-action, "whippy" rods are still responsible for many lost peacock giants each year. The limber staffs ideal for some North American species are not suitable for peacock. A medium-heavy action rod should be considered the minimal stiffness acceptable to tangle with a big peacock bass. The rod blank must have adequate backbone and/or leverage to properly set the big hooks and fight the fish.

Short rods have to overcome a leverage-deficiency in order to power a peacock away from heavy cover. A 6 1/2- or 7-foot heavy or medium-heavy action rod will surpass most problems in the hands of an experienced angler. I have used the Berkley Series One graphites in those two lengths and actions for several years and found them to be up to the task.

Rods that have minute fractures in them tend to come apart at the time of maximum stress, like when the giant is powering away one last time. Broken guides also have been known to come loose or nick the line at an inappropriate time. Unless the baggage handlers in the airports are careless (and they often are), those are potential problems that can be eliminated at home by careful inspection.

Reel drags can be a major problem. Equipment that is cheap, old or heavily used may not have the smooth drag that is needed for handling big peacock bass. Overhaul your gear and keep it maintained for best luck. On my last few trips, I've been using Abu-Garcia Morrum baitcasters which are perhaps the best reels on the market. They are high quality (and cost), precision made reels that best minimize potential problems with gears, drag, spool, etc.

Line Up For Action

Line is always suspect when a big peacock bass breaks off. Line too light or too old, or an inferior knot are often the culprits. Going after huge fish with light line is usually foolish. Naturally, the habitat and other water characteristics should dictate the line test to a certain extent.

Heavy cover and the potential for big peacock bass mean you should select the line suited for the job. Lines testing 25 and 30 pounds are advisable for fish up to ten pounds in dense timber cover for example. I've often seen novice North American anglers venture to South America with 15 pound test line and light rods in hopes of doing battle with a real heavyweight. That's not too smart, unless you are after one of my line class world records.

I've used lines testing from 4 pounds (when after one of my world records) to 100 pounds. My favorite line for topwater fare, 60-pound Berkley Ultramax, is no longer being produced. Fortunately, I was able

Line strength, stretch and performance is extremely critical when hooked up to a giant. While the author landed this 20 pounder on 10 pound test Trilene (while after a line-class world record), he normally employs 50 to 100 pound test lines. Don't believe that this is overkill. You would be very sorry, very soon in many of the waters mentioned in this book.

to stock a few spools prior to their discontinuing it a few years ago. Since then, I have found their 50-pound Fireline to be a very good topwater plug line. For trolling the Big Game Woodchoppers or other giant surface plugs, the 80-pound test is ideal.

When fishing large submerged baits, such as Pet Spoons, 6-inch minnow plugs, Super Traps or Magnum Rat-L-Traps, I usually prefer a monofilament. I like 40-pound test Trilene Big Game in a green fluorescent color for most applications in giant peacock waters having typical entanglements.

Line does have an extended shelf life, but many days in the sun or in varying temperature extremes can shorten its effectiveness severely. Repeated breaks with appropriate size line denote either poor knot tying or rotten line. After extensive use, some braids wear themselves down when the fibers cut into each other. Knot tying proficiency, even with braided line, is easily gained, but a rotten line must be replaced. The best knot that I have found for braids (and monofilaments) is the Palomar. It is easy to tie and has a near-100 percent strength.

Naturally, general wear and tear can deteriorate the strength of a monofilament line too. The abrasion may not be noticeable, but the smart angler will snip off the first six feet or so of his line after each substantial use. Prevention is the best insurance against the loss of a big peacock.

Terminal tackle can very easily fail around even mid-size peacock bass. Split rings, snaps, swivels or line ties on many plugs suitable for largemouth bass just can't cut it when put up against a peacock. The hardware can also become weak or may have a manufacturing defect (other than being too weak) not noticed beforehand. Again the stress on all equipment is maximum when a big peacock bass is hooked. Other equipment problems such as a rotten or broken net, boat seats not able to handle the strain during a battle, etc. are potential problems that you may face in South America.

Physical Shortcomings

A poor hook set is the most common cause of losing a big peacock on the way to the boat. I've watched anglers fail to set the hook into a fish going away with the lure. While many peacock bass hit so hard they set the hook themselves, strength and quick reflexes are vital to success.

A large topwater lure with one or two big tail props will "resist" a smooth hook set, even with low-stretch braid or other superline. Just the resistance of the water on the plug will slow down the acceleration in a hook set. Anglers that believe a light hook set is needed for lures with exposed treble hooks is sadly mistaken. He'll lose some big peacocks.

Failure to exert enough pressure to keep a big peacock bass away from any anchor rope, outboard or trolling motor, or out of dense cover could be the result of a physical shortcoming. That could also be the result of a mental lapse on the part of an angler, as I explained earlier. I've often seen big peacock bass take off in heavy cover and drive so deep into it that the angler never again saw the trophy.

Many guides will dive into the dark depths in pursuit of a brush-tangled peacock, but you normally have to be in control of the fish at all times to eventually land one.

Mental Lapses

The difference between a good fisherman and a bad one is usually not the ability to think. It is the ability to apply knowledge on the water. The good angler will be concentrating on what he is doing and thinking about what he will do if that big peacock bass strikes his lure on each retrieve.

In the heat of battle, a fishing partner will occasionally grab the line to assist in the landing of a trophy. At that time, the peacock bass has a shorter, more firm point to pull away from than a length of line running through the rod tip. It is often then that big peacock bass get away.

Another piece of advice is to never let an inexperienced partner or guide help you land the peacock bass by touching your line. Net help, if effective, is great, but too much can happen on a short, taut line if the fish is still energetic. Grabbing the line to lift the giant into the boat is dangerous indeed and can be costly.

Never try to "horse" a big peacock bass in waters with few obstructions. That's undue strain on the equipment. Conversely, never give the fish

I always have my guide release the giants so that another angler can have another battle down the road. Since we always release the big peacock bass after the battle, I try to lip-land them with either a Bogagrip or a Fish-On grabber. The Boga-grip can also weigh the fish. The net can cause loss of the protective slime coat and later infection on the fish, so I prefer not to use them. Since the lure in a thrashing fish mouth can easily entangle the net, don't ever use one on a small or mid-size fish. You can also use a gloved hand, or simply let the guide grab the fish. Peacocks have raspy teeth which can draw blood if lipped sans protection. Once landed, it is important to take pictures, measurements and weight quickly and then immediately release the fish.

slack line. It will usually spit out the hook or use the extra length to wrap around an obstruction and break the line. Both situations occur to many anglers during the heat of battle. For more detailed strategies for battling peacock bass, see chapter 14 in my book, "Peacock Bass Explosions".

Catch-And-Release

As noted earlier, when the guide does use the net, he'll hopefully net the peacock bass head first. Trying to net a "green" fish from the tail end is a major cause of lost trophies at boatside.

It is very important to understand the correct way to release a big peacock. Conservation of the peacock bass resource is vital. As opposed to largemouth bass, most peacocks cannot take the stress of being out of water a long time. Be sure to revive in shallow water any fish that doesn't immediately swim off when placed back in the water. That fish may be over-stressed.

Peacocks are a precious commodity. Even a tired fish that swims away is not out of danger. Piranhas, dolphins and other predators may go after the over-stressed peacock. The danger in the deep comes in many forms, as was proven on one of my trips to the Amazonia Region.

On a few occasions, I've hooked a small peacock only to have piranhas eat half of it on the way to the boat.

My partner Rodolfo Fernandez and I had caught and released three 15-pounders in a small lake off the Jufari River. We had done well and released all in, what we thought, was perfect health. But this story is a sad one. One of the big guys didn't fare well, as we found out later.

While having lunch, I noticed what looked like an animal or big fish on the surface a few hundred yards away. We motored over to a struggling fish and netted it. It was one that we had caught earlier. Every fin, plus several chunks from the meaty part of the tail, had been eaten off by piranhas. The giant peacock had no propulsion or stabilization, so it floundered on its side, at the mercy of the piranhas. It's normal for the piranhas to nibble on a struggling peacock's lower tail and anal fins.

The moral of this is to emphasize the importance of releasing a big fish quickly and while it is strong. If there is any doubt, take it to the shallows for release and recuperation. Piranhas generally don't inhabit super shallow waters.

Once you have successfully landed, measured, photographed and released your catch, you may want the ultimate memento, a replica. Don Frank is probably the world's best taxidermist specializing in all species of fish including giant peacock bass and payara. He has done a couple of outstanding replicas for me, and I highly recommend him. His contact information mentioned in my first book, "Peacock Bass Explosions", has been changed. He can now be reached at 5012 Five Corners Road, Smithville, MO 64089 or phone (816) 532-3500.

Knowing many of the potential causes of losing big peacock bass, I doubt if I'll ever lose another. Ha! Want to bet?

Chapter 14

RANGE/SEASONAL MOVEMENTS

Understanding the seasons and the range

The natural range of the peacock bass is the Amazon, Orinoco and Rio Negro basins, a latitudinal range of about 28 degrees or over 1800 miles. They are adaptable and in fact, have been introduced into many waters around the world. Today, you can fish for them in three places - Florida, Hawaii and Puerto Rico - without even needing a passport.

Peacock bass can now be found in Panama, and I'm told by good authority, in Costa Rica. While the biggest of these bruisers still live in Venezuela, Brazil and Colombia, other countries, such as Guyana, Surinam, French Guiana, Ecuador, Peru and Bolivia, have waters that abound with peacock bass. For more detail on names and ranges, review the information in my first book, "Peacock Bass Explosions."

Peacock bass have been introduced in reservoirs in southeast Brazil and in the Pantanal region in areas outside the Amazonas. Some noteworthy spots in southern Brazil include Rio Piqueiri, Lago Itumbiara, Rio Paranaiba, Lago Sao Simao, Lago Agua Vermelha, Ilha Solteira, Furnas, Marimbondo and Volt Grande. Gray bar peacocks up to 10 pounds are taken from the submerged timber in Lake Itumbiara, but strong winds can sometimes affect fishing.

Fishing for schools of small yellow peacocks takes place during the winter in clear water weedbeds mid-way up the Agua Vermelha. Lago Sao Simao lies on the Paranaiba River above the intersection of the Grande River which together forms the Parana River. Blue peacock and yellow peacock are taken there from deep structures and weedbeds.

Friend Ron Looi, who has the "Peacock Bass Page" on the internet, was partially responsible for their introduction into several small ponds in Malaysia. He reports that peacocks have been bred for the aquarium trade for years in Taiwan and Indonesia. One reservoir in Singapore has been stocked perhaps unintentionally with peacock, according to Looi.

Bolivia, one of the last frontiers left in South America, may provide a new opportunity for peacock bass chasers. One outfitter is trying to establish an operation on the Yati and Paragua Rivers in south-central Bolivia, 200 miles northeast of Santa Cruz. Another has an area with both peacock and golden dorado that I'm anxious to try.

Another area that I'm anxious to try is Guyana's Highland rivers and Savannah lakes. The Essequibo and its major tributary, the Rupununi, are black water rivers with head waters in the Guyana Highlands along the borders with Brazil and Venezuela. The sandy-bottomed streams flow through the Rupununi savannahs where several blackwater natural lakes provide excellent fishing for peacock bass (called "lukunani" here). A few ranches in the area provide very rustic guest facilities, meals, boat and motor and local Amerindian guides at very reasonable prices.

The Essequibo and its tributaries, like the Rewa, offer a variety of species in like sizes, along with excellent giant payara fishing, pacu, piranha, imara, bicuda, surubim, matrinxa and sardinata. A motorized float trip with primitive tent camping is offered by one outfitter. There are very few lagoons, so fishing is primarily in the rivers and below the numerous rapids and small falls. Amerindian guides easily portage the boats through these obstacles. The upper tributaries are uninhabited except for a few small native villages.

The very best locations providing the top action often change from one year to the next, or even one month to the next. That's why it is important to keep in touch with the fishing tour operators that offer trips to South America.

The movement and behavior of the fish varies in different habitats and water types. Much of the knowledge of such is based on actual experience fishing for the peacock in a vast assortment of locations and habitat. Very few biological studies on the species have been conducted, and it is fair to say that the fishery database is years behind all North American game fish. Sport fishing in South America is a relatively new concept, one that is however, taking giant leaps forward each year.

The Amazon's Rainy Season

Temperatures vary little in the tropics, so seasons are generally based on rainfall. There are two so-called "seasons" in Brazil's Amazonia Region: the wet season and the dry season (or fishing season). The two seasons affect all fisheries in the rainforest, but the timing of those

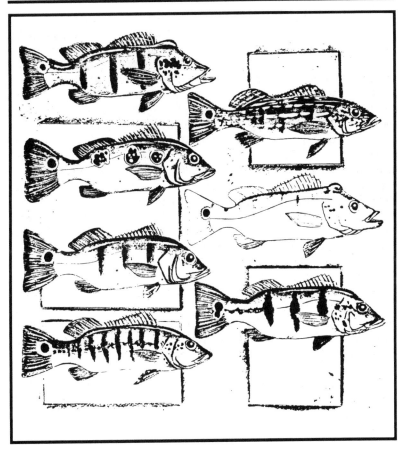

Figure 5 - Peacock bass come in a variety of species and perhaps, subspecies. Their patterns and coloration may in part depend on their age and environmental factors additionally. Some biologists believe there are three species, while others have identified 15 or so. In my travels, I have observed what I believe to be around 8 or 9 unique peacock bass. Call them species, hybrids, subspecies or "members of the same family." This drawing from my first book, "Peacock Bass Explosions", identifies, (from the top to the bottom), the grande or three-bar peacock, the speckled, the butterfly, the gray-bar or five-bar, another 3-bar version of the butterfly, the hybrid, and the intermedia or royal peacock.

Resacas or oxbow lakes found off river bends are inundated during high water times, as the runoff goes several miles into the Amazon region jungles.

seasons vary depending on where the watershed is precisely located. Some areas may be in the midst of their rainy season while others are enjoying dry times.

The nature of the runoff, the length of its tributaries, the distance from the Equator and the surrounding land masses all influence the cycling of the seasons and add to the complexity of determining the best time for fishing. My Peacock Bass Calendar attempts to define the "typical", optimal timing for various fish locations.

The wet season usually starts with occasional afternoon showers for a few weeks and then heavy downpours occur most days for at least a couple of months before they subside. The rivers and lakes rise and overflow from the torrential rains into the surrounding floodplain. Inundated areas attract feeding baitfish.

High water is bad news for peacock bass fishermen, so knowing the water levels prior to the trip can make a big difference in enjoying a productive adventure or wisely canceling an undoubtedly unsuccessful trip. During high water, peacock bass move into the flooded forest or "iguapos" to feed on the forage fish and to live.

Most waters fluctuate substantially over the year. Larger tributaries may rise 50 feet and spread out 50 miles or more during the maximum rainfall. In the wet seasons, water levels can rise 10 or 12 feet in a week on some tributaries blowing away any fishing opportunity. An increase of 3 or 4 feet in a day or two during the dry season might do the same.

The Amazon's Dry Season

At the end of the wet season, it normally takes a few months of dry weather for the water levels to fall to productive heights. As the water

During the low water "dry" season, catches like the author's 19-pound Agua Boa peacock lifted by guide Cinval Gutierre are possible. During the rainy season, such fish are impossible to locate.

levels drop, first in the headwaters and then downstream, peacock bass forage are forced out of the jungles and into the lagoons and rivers. The peacock follow and are then accessible to the sportfisherman. The dry season typically means waters within their banks and peacock bass in habitat that can be fished.

An angler typically has 3 or 4 months of fishable water levels but El Nino and/or other factors can affect that. Even in the dry season, an occasional shower in the "rain" forest may soak you while on the water. Remember it rains in the rainforest.

Daily downpours may occur up to half the year. Late rains during the beginning of the dry season or "off-year" rains in the middle of the dry season can cause problems. Peacocks may scatter into the flooded jungle timber and again become difficult to catch.

*T*he *dry season often means rivers get extremely shallow and navigation becomes difficult at times, but rewards for accessing deeper waters are usually great. The author will wade a mile to catch a giant peacock!*

In a "normal" dry season, larger peacocks may take up residence in deeper water away from the shallow shoreline. They often will move into the thin water to feed. Mid-size to smaller peacocks will generally cavort around the shallows and submerged structures near deep water in the dry season.

Critical Water Conditions

The exact nature of the Amazon tributary watershed determines the prime months and the length of prime fishing. In fact, some waterways have only a couple of months of good fishing potential in the best of times and conditions. Generally speaking, the best period north of the Amazon River may be between November and April, while in the south, it is often between July and January.

Timing of your trip is critical to success. Additional tips on planning are detailed in chapter 16 in "Peacock Bass Explosions" and in chapter 14 of "Peacock Bass & Other Fierce Exotics". A Peacock Trip Checklist is included in the following chapter.

The very best dry season waters in the Amazonia Region are those called "black water." If the lagoons have relatively clear, tannin-stained water, which the adjoining rivers normally do not, the best peacock fishing will be in the lagoons. In normal conditions, the larger peacock bass haunt the lakes and coves off the river channel during the dry season. In low water and minimal current conditions, peacocks may even concentrate around huge rocks or in deep pools in the river.

SEASONAL CALENDAR

Range	Jan	Feb	Mar	Apr	May	Jun	Jul	Aug	Sep	Oct	Nov	Dec
Peru Am.Hd	HR	HR	HR	HR	H	D	DL	DL	SLS	R	HR	HR
Brazil												
Am SW	R	HR	HR	HR	HR	H	D	DL	DLS	DLS	DL	R
Am SE	HR	HR	HR	H	D	DL	DLS	DLS	DL	L	R	RH
Am Cen	HR	HR	HR	HR	H	H	D	DL	DLS	DL	L	R
Am NW	DLS	DLS	DL	L	R	R	HR	HR	HR	D	DL	DL
Am NE	R	HR	HR	HR	HR	HR	H	D	DL	DLS	L	R
Pantan.	HR	HR	HR	H	D	DL	DLS	DLS	DL	L	R	RH
Venezuela												
So Rio	DL	DLS	L	HR	HR	HR	HR	HR	HR	H	D	DL
SW Rio	DL	DL	DLS	DLS	LS	R	HR	HR	HR	HR	D	DL
Guri L	DL	DL	DLS	DS	HR	HR	HR	HR	HR	HR	DL	DL
Panama												
L. Gatun	D	DS	DS	D	R	R	HR	HR	HR	HR	D	D
U.S.												
So. FL	DL	DLS	DLS	DL	LR	LR	LR	LR	L	L	DL	DL
Hawaii	HR	HR	H	H	S	LS	LS	L	L	L	R	R
P. Rico	DL	DL	DL	DL	L	S	S	RS	RS	R	L	L
Colombia												
E. Rios	DL	DLS	DL	L	L	R	HR	HR	HR	H	D	DL

Legend: R-Rainy Season, D-Dry Season, S-Spawning, H-High Water, L-Low Water.

Note: the shaded calendar period is the typical "fishing season"

Hitting the water levels right can lead to big numbers and big fish. The author's prime-time giant shown here weighed almost 17 pounds. Fish like this disappear when water conditions aren't right.

Seasonal Calendar

The peacock bass responds differently in the different, "normal" calendar periods. Unusual high water or extremely low water can occur during certain periods throughout the year as affected by drought and other atypical weather influences. The "normal" periods are obviously based on nature's clock and can vary as much as 8 or 10 weeks from one year to the next. Spawning may occur anywhere from one month into and after through the dry season, but it has little affect on the overall fishing success.

Calendar periods also vary by tributary within a region, depending on its watershed and other factors. One or more Amazon tributaries in Northeast Brazil, for example, may be enjoying their end of season low water period and excellent fishing, while the majority of tributaries in that region are high with substantial runoff and lousy fishing.

Chapter 15

TACKLE/EQUIPMENT CONSIDERATIONS

Peacock Bass Strategies For Success

When you travel to remote fishing operations, you have to carry along optimal tackle for the species. While most travelers to the Amazon are after peacock bass, the other giants pretty much require similar gear. Your tackle should be sturdy and up to the task of handling wild, aggressive fish which will often range from 5 to over 20 pounds.

Most tackle choices depend on the size of fish to be encountered. Keep in mind however, that neither peacock bass, nor most of the other exotic species swimming in Amazon, are spooked by line size or color, or anything else for that matter. For some detail, I've included a couple of very specific charts which I believe offer well-intentioned guidance, based on my 40 or so trips after peacock bass around the world.

Following also are some "general" guidelines and suggestions on rods, reels, lines and lures. Consider the largest sizes of lines and lures when fishing areas where 20 pound peacock bass range and the smaller sizes in waters where they may grow only to 10 or 12 pounds. The same goes for payara and golden dorado fishermen and anglers after some of the other sportfish of South America's rain forest.

For maximum power and optimal control, baitcasting outfits are recommended for peacock bass fishermen after all sizes of fish. Accurate casting is vital in some areas of dense cover or surroundings. For the giants, use a quality, high-speed casting reel with good ball bearing gears and smooth (properly adjusted) drag mounted on heavy-action, straight-handle baitcasting rods. My favorite reels are the lightweight, one-piece Abu-Garcia Morrums in the M5600C and M6600C models.

A 6 1/2 to 7-foot medium-heavy action rod with lure capacity rating of up to 1 1/2 ounces is appropriate for peacock bass up to 20 pounds,

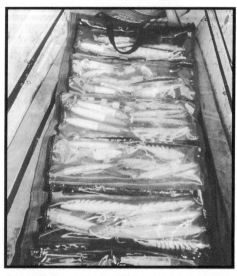

A large selection of big baits is a requirement if you are chasing giant peacocks. Soft tackle bags or individual boxes in a soft case are ideal for use in South America. Not all small tackle boxes hold the right size lures.

depending on the line being employed. The Berkley Series One graphite B50-7'MH rod is a good one for most uses in peacock country. The multi-ball bearing casting reel is most suitable for tossing the big plugs and landing the giant fish.

A traveler should take a minimum of 3 baitcasting outfits, because things happen in the jungle. I'll normally have 5 or 6 carefully-selected rods and reels along on most of my jaunts to the remote areas.

Spool your baitcaster with a heavy fused line, such as 50 pound test Fireline which is a great all-around line for most applications in the Amazon. Also have a backup rig or two with 60- to 100-pound break strength braid, and one with a quality 25- to 40-pound monofilament, such as Trilene Big Game solar mono. Use the mono for the submergent presentations, and use nothing smaller if you want to land the trophy of your dreams.

The strong, low-stretch and limber superline is required for effectively fishing large topwater plugs. You want a "direct" response from the lure when you jerk the rod tip. A monofilament with lots of stretch causes the lure to react slowly and makes setting up a good cadence very difficult. The topwater tailspinner plug should move about two feet at a time leaving a roostertail and making a sound such as "schoop", pause, "schoop".

The best knot to use for most applications and most lines is the Palomar. Keep the hooks honed sharp and re-check them after each fish

*F*or giant peacock, a powerful rod and reel and large plugs with substantial hook/hardware are necessary. Extra heavy line with minimal terminal tackle is preferred by the author. A selection of Larry's top lures would include topwaters as well as a few submergent plug and spoon options.

and hang-up. Also check the alignment of the lure hooks and any tailspinner that may have been bent by an aggressive peacock or by your cast against a tree or rock.

Luring Thoughts

Peacock bass generally like large lures and a fast, noisy retrieve. They love to smash topwater baits, and such lures are productive on oversized fish about 90 percent of the time. Use big surface baits for giant peacocks. The most productive plugs for monster peacocks are those that weigh 1 to 2 ounces and measure 6 to 8 inches long.

Top water, tail-spinner plugs, like the Luhr-Jensen Big Game Woodchopper, the double-propped Amazon Ripper and the Magnum Jerkin' Sam are very effective "dinner bell ringers" for peacock bass larger than 12 pounds. The latter two lack a treble near the head of the plug, so I often employ the single-prop, three-hook Woodchopper. Make sure to remove the front propeller of any Woodchopper that you want to toss on the heavy tackle. Some come from the factory with it already removed.

Big lures do catch giant fish. The author's specially-designed 14 inch long Woodchopper has caught over 15 big guys, and the smallest was over 9 pounds!

The most productive retrieve is usually jerk-pause-jerk. I'll use the rod tip to move the lure, and reel in slack at each pause. That keeps the line taut, ready to set the hook at any time. Peacocks will often swirl behind a topwater plug or slap at it with their body and not get hooked. They may come back and hit the lure that continues its cadence across the surface or lose interest.

Ideal plug sizes overall for the majority of locales range from about 3/4- to 2-ounces and lengths from 5 to 8 inches. Lure hardware on all artificials should be saltwater strength as a minimum or have existing hooks replaced with extra-strong hooks and heavy duty split rings. I recommend VMC 4/0 No. 7626BZ Conecut, 4X Heavy Musky Treble hooks as replacement hardware for lures attracting peacocks weighing between 13 and 25 pounds. A double-digit peacock can straighten out some 4/0, 3x treble hooks, open up the strongest split ring and pull a 2-inch-long screw out of an 8-inch-long wooden topwater bait.

The trophy-seeking angler should have rigged in the boat, ready to cast, several of the giant tail-prop topwaters to "rip" across the surface, a 6- or 7-inch-long minnow-type jerkbait that runs just under the surface with a moderately fast retrieve, a giant 5-inch-long spoon with Berkley Ball Bearing Size 3, 125-pound test Cross-Lok snap swivel for slow, probing retrieves, and a giant vibrating plug or lipless crankbait to seek out monster peacocks in the depths. If you insist on using normal 1/2- to 3/4-ounce bass lures for peacock bass that may weigh from 8 to 20 pounds, replace the hooks and split rings with extra-strong saltwater terminal tackle.

Magnum Rat-L-Traps, Super Traps and Brute Sugar Shad offer a good change of pace from tossing the giant surface baits, and they will attract most giants that swim deeper in jungle waters. At times, a peacock will be reluctant to explode on a surface lure. Large, shallow or mid-depth jerkbaits, such as those made by PRADCO, Storm, UKKO and Luhr-Jensen, work well in riverine areas on a variety of big fish. They too are a relief for tired arms, shoulder, and back and for blistered hands.

Large, single hook spoons, such as the #18 Accetta Pet Spoon, and heavy white jigs are sometimes perfect for dredging less aggressive fish from the depths. Such submerged lures retrieved slowly with a few intermittent jerks often trigger strikes from those fish that are somewhat tentative. You may not experience the audio and visual impact of the surface strike, but you will be in on the powerful battles of the fish. It is often wise to use a variety of lures to achieve the anticipated results of the fishing trip.

Prime Places

The biggest peacock bass and other exotics of the Amazon often hang out around boulders and rocks blocking swift water, in the lagoons off the river, in front of small, tributary creeks, behind islands, off sandbars and in deadfall-laden outer bends. Therefore, hangups and breakoffs may be a problem.

When fishing rapid-flowing water, cast upstream and work the bait between any rocks and then into the eddy behind them. Most larger peacock will hang out at the edge of the fast water and not in it. Smaller, faster peacock, especially those speckled with the white or yellow horizontal dashes, may be in the swift areas. Be prepared for a unique battle in current and in the sharp-edged rocks, and be prepared for discovering a concentration of peacocks in such habitat.

Lagoons are my favorite waters, and the prime peacock locations in them vary. Some lagoons have it all: deadfalls, rocks, depth, points, sand bars, ditches and creeks, and flooded timber. Others have little other than open water, where some giants do exist. I and most other addicted peacock bass chasers have caught the vast majority of our fish from lagoons and lakes, including land-locked, oxbow-type and those connected by small cuts.

The top spot in shallow lagoons is often at their mouth or "boca" from the river. In mid-deep (4 to 8 feet) to deep (8 to 16 feet) lagoons, points with some form of wood (or boulders) are top producers. Fish the deepest side of any point first and then cast beyond the point and retrieve your bait perpendicular to it. Then, run the bait parallel along the point or ridge. Then work the other side of the point throughly.

As waters drop in the dry season, the mid-deep lagoons become shallow and oftentimes have limited boat access. Big fish are then found in the mouth of the lake or right in the middle, if sufficient depth (4 to 6 feet) exits. Although more common along the rivers, sand bars are exposed and any deep pockets behind them then yield lots of big peacock.

Deep lagoons often have big fish swimming in the middle, where a properly presented lure will draw a strike. Trolling the giant topwater plugs or some of the submergent fare will often be productive on the biggest of peacocks. Many times, I have cast my lure away from the bank into the middle of a lagoon and hooked up with a giant fish. This is especially true when the shore habitat is producing only small fish; the giants control the deep water in the middle!

Bank On Them

Any large laydowns should draw a few casts. Peacocks love timber and the more dense the limb structure, the more concentrated they may be. The very largest limbs often attract the biggest peacocks. Similarly, a large stand of flooded trees in one part of the lagoon may concentrate big fish and lots of them. I remember one afternoon taking 3 peacocks, each weighing in the upper "teens", from one such wooded flats area.

Fish will often follow lures out of cover before striking them, and it's then you may see the characteristic "V" wake right behind your surface plug. This is expecially true in shallow water where they may be a little tentative about smashing the bait. They want a little depth under them, before they blast the plug sometimes. If the water is clear, you may even see two or three peacocks chase the lure and then the strike, and excitement doesn't get much better than that.

Another great opportunity to catch peacock is in shallow water when they are chasing bait and feeding aggressively. I have caught many peacocks that have given themselves away first. I always scan the surface for any activity, even a dimple. I once threw to a single, tiny surface dimple in the middle of a lagoon and caught a 15 pound plus peacock. I have also thrown into tremendous commotion of a school of very big peacocks violently tearing up a school of baitfish and not drawn a strike. Fortunately, the latter is rare.

On several occasions, I have seen baitfish knocked from or ejected from the shallows to land on the bank and kick in an attempt to reenter the water. I once watched a peacock during the course of a battle, spit up a dead baitfish. I cast to and around that floating forage about 20 times before giving up on its drawing power. I thought that another peacock might be checking it out, and sure enough, when my casts stopped I saw the dead baitfish disappear in the mouth of another peacock!

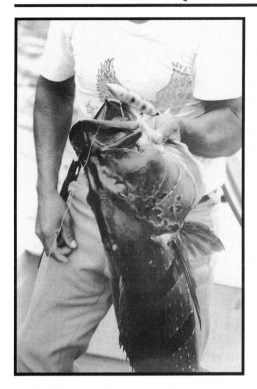

To effectively land the giants, use a hook file frequently to hone the large trebles on the topwater plugs to razor sharpness

Planning Ahead

Bring plenty of line and bring steel leaders for the toothy critters (which include everything except peacock bass) that will try to carry your tackle away. Slashers, like the payara, often put pin holes in the minnow baits, so carry extra lures in the tackle box. When fishing spinning-type lures such as spoons, use a strong ball bearing swivel to prevent line twist.

The most appropriate time to employ a snap is when you want to add a small protective buffer above the lure without going to a steel leader. I usually suggest using a snap swivel with a Rat-L-Trap, because it is also an effective lure for a lot of other sportfish which have sharp teeth. I sometimes use a very effective pull-and-pause retrieve when fishing the Super Trap, Magnum Trap and Brute Sugar Shad, but I found out many years ago, that piranha would strike at the plug on the fall and cut the line near the tie eye. Using a snap/swivel has eliminated that problem for the most part.

TABLE OF LURE RECOMMENDATIONS

Lure/Mfg.	Size(oz)	Snap	Swivel	Comments
Woodchopper/ Luhr-Jensen	1 7/8	no	no	Superline only, single tailspinner only
Amazon Ripper/ Luhr-Jensen	1 3/4	no	no	Superline only
Mag.Jerk'n Sam/ Luhr-Jensen	1 3/4	no	no	Low stretch line only
Top Dog/ Mirr-O-Lure	3/4	yes	no	Great castibility and durability
Red Fin (7")/ Cordell	1	yes	no	Great "come-back" lure, excellent for trolling
Javelin/ Luhr-Jensen	1 1/4	yes	no	Follow-up lure, sturdy
PJ Shiner/ Luhr-Jensen	5/8	yes	no	Replace hooks & split ring for midsize fish
Magnum Long A/ Bomber	1 3/4	yes	no	Great trolling plug
J'ntdThunderstick/ Storm	5/8	yes	no	Sturdy hardware, tough body
Super Trap/ Bill Lewis	1 1/2	yes	yes	For 6-15 feet of water and giant peacock
Mag. Force Trap/ Bill Lewis	1	yes	yes	Great all-around lure for most situations
Sugar Shad Brute/ Luhr-Jensen	5/8	yes	yes	For mid-size fish, strong hooks
Frenzy Rattl'r Berkley	1/2	yes	yes	For mid-size fish, change out hooks
Accetta Pet Spoon Luhr-Jensen	(#18)	yes	yes	Great bait for trolling and casting to swirls
Krocodile Spoon/ Luhr-Jensen	3/4	yes	yes	Ideal for rivers & rocks
Frenzy Diver' Berkley	7/8	yes	no	Medium Mag model for mid-size fish

Lure color doesn't seem to be a huge variable in the scheme of things when after peacock bass. Most of the super-aggressive fish want to come after anything in their territory, regardless of color, size or shape. They are intent on destroying that which has disturbed their peace and quiet. I have often commented that you could tie any color of noisy, surface-disturbing lure to a bright yellow rope and catch peacock bass.

The typical color of most of the lures in my tackle box are red-and-white, clown (yellow with dots), orange-and-black, firetiger, and silver-and-blue. I also have several topwaters that have a "peacock bass" color scheme. The proper tuning of the lures so that they run right is usually more important than color.

Another couple of items that can be very handy on a trip to "destructive" fish waters are a bottle of fingernail polish and some SuspenStrips or SuspenDots. The former is used to cover up and re-seal paint chips out of your plugs which will eventually be torn up by a few big peacock. Wood plugs with chunks of paint chewed off will quickly absorb water which may throw off the balance of the lure.

The SuspenDot System by Storm Lures are peel-off and stick-on adhesive weights. They can be used to make a lure heavier and cast further on the heavy line that is vital to withstand the peacock's legendary strike and runs, and they can also be employed to cover-up some of the chips, scares and holes made in the bait, which will help re-seal areas prone to soaking up water. Put enough SuspenStrips on a small floating lure (with dry surface), and it's easier to toss on heavy tackle.

While natural baits such as lambari, pula-pula, or durinho (shiners) can be effective for peacock, they are usually not employed by American anglers. In fact, very few of the South American opearations catering to U.S. travelers have much experience with such. If you do wish to try for a giant catfish with cut, natural bait after dark, do take some heavy-duty hooks in 5/0 to 8/0 sizes and several one-ounce lead weights.

Equipment For The Expedition

Several equipment items are vital to any peacock bass expedition. They are: a pair of long-nose pliers, a knife, a pair of light-colored gloves, a scale and a measuring tape. You'll need line clippers and a hook file or hone to keep the hooks as sharp as possible.

Perhaps the most utilitarian fish tool ever invented is the innovative BogaGrip which is made by Eastaboga Tackle, 261 Mudd St., Eastaboga, AL 36260 or phone (256) 831-9682. The highly recommended instrument is a fish handler which can land, lift and quickly and accurately weigh fish up to 30 pounds with one hand without ever touching it. Take one

TABLE OF TECHNIQUE/EQUIPMENT RECOMMENDATIONS

Technique (Equip)	Size of Fish (max)	Reel & Rod	Line (lb.) type	Lure type	Wt. (oz)
Casting	7-10 lb.	quality baitcast 6 1/2 ft. MH	50 Fireline 30 Big Game	Jerkin'Sam topwaters	1 3/4-1
Casting	7-10 lb.	quality baitcast 6 1/2 ft. MH	50 Fireline 30 Big Game	jerkbaits spoons	1/2-1 3/4-1
Casting	7-10 lb.	quality baitcast 6 1/2 ft. MH	25 Big Game 50-75 braid 30 mono	Mag. Trap vibrators	1 1/2-3/4
Spinning	7-10 lb.	quality spinning 6-6 1/2 ft. M/MH	20-25 mono	vibrators crankbaits	1/2-3/4 7/8
Casting	13-15 lb.	quality baitcast 6 1/2-7 ft. MH/H	50 Fireline 30-40 BigGame 70-90 braid	Amaz.Ripper Woodchopper topwaters	11/4 11/4
Casting	13-15 lb.	quality baitcast 6 1/2-7 ft. MH	50 Fireline 30-40 BigGame	jerkbaits spoons	3/4+ 3/4+
Casting	13-15 lb.	quality baitcast 6 1/2-7 ft. MH	50 Fireline 30-40 BigGame	vibrators	1+
Trolling	13-15 lb.	lg-capacity b/c 6 1/2-7 ft. MH/H	50-90 braid 30-40 BigGame	topwaters jerkbaits spoon,vibr.	1+ 1+ 3/4+
Casting	20-25 lb.	quality baitcast 6 1/2-7 ft. MH/H	50-80 Fireline 60-100 braid	Amaz..Ripper Woodchopper	1+ 1+
Casting	20-25 lb.	quality baitcast 6 1/2-7 ft. MH/H	50-80 Fireline 60-100 braid	topwaters Super Trap	1+ 1+
Casting	20-25 lb.	quality baitcast 6 1/2-7 ft. MH/H	50Fireline 30-40 BigGame	jerkbaits spoons	1+ 7/8+
Trolling	20-25 lb.	lg-capacity b/c 6 1/2-7 ft. H	80 Fireline 40 BigGame 80-100 braid	topwaters jerkbaits spoon,vibr.	1+ 1+ 3/4+

of these with you and you won't need a net, gloves or additional scale. The tool is designed to reduce the "out-of-water" time and to promote "catch and release" fishing without overstressing or injurying the fish, according to co-owner Gary Alldredge. And, you know that catch and release is one of my goals in this lifetime.

Another must is an insect repellent with deet. While I have encountered few insects on the majority of my trips to blackwater river areas in South America, I do remember a few with an overabundance of

The Boga Grip is a fish handling device that also weighs the catch. Using such a tool to handle a peacock prior to release will help conserve the peacock fishery, and your hand.

"no-see-ums". Peruvian waters are usually brownwater rivers that are high in nutrients and, unfortunately, insect life. Their blackwater lagoons are often isolated from the main currents of the rivers in the very interesting country.

Since it is wise to limit your skin's exposure to deet, try to locate a controlled-release repellent. Sawyer and other manufacturers make good ones. Use a lotion on the skin and a spray on clothing for added protection. If you use a separate sunblock lotion, apply it about 10 minutes prior to the insect repellent application for best results.

Travel Tips

Whether you are going to Brazil after giant peacock bass or to South Florida after some of their rapidly-growing butterfly peacocks, you need to be prepared. What you take along should be well thought out. Your tour operator will keep you appraised of required travel documentation and restrictions.

Clothing for most of the fishing trips to peacock destinations should be light weight and light colored and comfortable in the to-be-expected heat and humidity. A pair of quality polarized sunglasses, long-sleeved

☒ PEACOCK TRIP CHECKLIST

Tickets
Passport
Visa (for Brazil)
Tourist card
Tip money
Health precautions
   medications, pills
   first aid kit
Light weight clothing
   long sleeve shirts
   long pants
   wide-brimmed hat
Sunscreen (SPF 30 or 45)
Polarized sunglasses
Deet insect repellent
Rain gear
Windbreaker
Gloves, thumb guard
Waterproof gear bag
Zip-loc/trash bags
Flashlight (w/batteries)

Heavy-duty rod case
Carry-on bag
Camera, film
Spanish/English phrase book,
   electronic translator, or the
   LOP Portugese/English
   Translation Sheet
"Peacock Bass Explosions" book
"Peacock Bass & Other Fierce
   Exotics" book
Appropriate Tackle
   rods, reels,
   long-nose pliers
   knife, hook file
   scale, measuring tape
   lip-lock grabber or
      BogaGrip
   line clippers
   extra treble hooks
   replacement line
   split ring pliers

cotton shirts, long pants and a wide-brimmed hat are wise to protect yourself from the sun (and bug bites).

Use sunscreen for your exposed face, neck and hands. Take lightweight rain gear, a windbreaker, a small first aid kit and a flashlight. For additional tips and information, addicts should check out the first two peacock bass books in this series!

Chapter 16

TOP FLY ACTION ADVICE

A collection of flies no peacock flyfisher should be without

Flies do catch peacocks, and sometimes the action can be non-stop, as I found out on one of my ventures to a tributary off Brazil's Rio Negro. South American fly fishing expert Rodolfo Fernandez and I had outboard problems one morning and had drifted against a shallow creek bank. While our guide worked on the motor, Fernandez waved his long wand a few times and started catching small "paca" or speckled peacock about 10 feet from the boat. Every short drift of the fly downcurrent in the four-foot deep water brought a strike and a peacock.

While the size of the fish left a lot to be desired, he and I both enjoyed the action during our "downtime". The outboard was again running in about 20 minutes, and we headed off to bigger fish and bigger tales. Who knows how long the one-a-minute bites right beside the boat would have continued?

I have caught peacocks on a fly (notice that it is plural), but I am far, far from being an expert. However, I do know several expert fly fishermen who have extensive experience putting various fly patterns in front of peacock bass. I have fished with several "fly guys" and have "picked their brains" for the information presented in this chapter and, of course, for enhanced credibility in this area.

Garrett VeneKlasen, J. W. Smith, Howard McKinney and Rodolfo Fernandez are all fly fishing addicts with plenty of time on the jungle waters that harbor the peacock bass. I asked each to reveal the most productive fly in their kit and how it is most effectively fished for catching big peacock bass. Their insight and advice should help all fly

Tying peacock flies right in camp is one way to always have plenty of the right patterns. Rodolfo Fernandez (shown) and Garrett VeneKlasen tie their favorites as needed.

fishermen do a better job of locating and catching their quarry. Here's a great collection of peacock bass flies!

Garrett's Brycon

For over a decade, Garrett VeneKlasen has experimented extensively with fly patterns for peacock bass. Several challenges present themselves to the fly caster, according to the avid fly fisherman, the first and foremost being size.

"Trophy peacocks prefer to eat extremely large baitfish," he says. "In fact the 'bait' that trophy peacocks eat are the only thing you're apt to catch if you use a fly smaller than 4-5-inches. I repeatedly have 10-pound-plus peacocks eat smaller butterfly peacocks that are hooked at the end of my line. With this in mind, big flies are the norm for me rather than the exception."

Another consideration for VeneKlasen is the tying material. A durable, lifelike material that presents as large a silhouette as possible without sacrificing 'castability' is required. The expert flytier has tried a variety. Rabbit fur looks great in the water, but casts like a wet rag. Saddle hackle works fairly well, but can't hold up to a peacock's punishing antics.

"I've tried dozens of the latest synthetics and still have not found one that suits my needs," he admits. "The problem with synthetics is that

A great collection of peacock bass flies by the world's best fly fishing addicts would include Garrett's Brycon (top R), the Peacock Deceiver (top L), the Flash-Tail Whistler (bottom L), and the Ariramba Fly (bottom R.).

they either tangle around the hook (or in the peacock's teeth) or they're too stiff and hamper the fly's action. In the end, what I have settled with is jumbo bucktail. This comparatively inexpensive material comes in every color under the rainbow, has an unbeatable action in the water and takes an impressive beating."

"I follow a couple of simple rules as far as color choice is concerned," explains VeneKlasen. "Water clarity, stain and light intensity dictate what color fly I use. If I'm fishing in off-colored green or heavily tannin-stained rivers during intense light conditions, I'll use either a red/yellow or black/yellow fly with plenty of flash to them. If the light is low, I'll switch to a black/white or dark blue/white fly with little or no flash."

"Eyes are not necessary if the water is off color," he continues. "Clear water color combinations are usually a mix of white, olive, gray and red or burnt orange. There are also a couple of 'Angel Fish' variations which work quite well. I have found that big prism eyes drastically increase strikes in clear water."

Tying Instructions for Garrett's Brycon (Amazon Annie)

VeneKlasen opts for a 5/0 Mustad #9174 Live Bait hook; a big peacock will easily straighten anything less stout, he contends.

Step 1: Before tying, always sharpen the point and bend the tip of the barb down only at the very end leaving a notable lump. If the barb is totally flattened, the hook will often slip out should a hooked fish manage to slacken your line.

Step 2: The goofy looking, high visibility tail serves two functions: it adds both action and length to the fly. To make the tail, simply cut off a five-inch section of 50-pound stiff monofilament and melt a small bump on one end to keep the bucktail from sliding off. Secure the melted end into your vise.

Step 3: Put a small drop of Super Glue (Duro) onto the mono right next to the where it's secured in the vise, then wrap on the thread. Use super-heavy moncore, so you can torque it down on the bucktail without breaking off. The tail is tied in with one clump of bucktail and soaked in Super Glue. Remove the tail section from the vise.

Step 4: After sharpening/de-barbing the hook, roughen a small area directly behind the eye prior to starting the thread. This ensures that the thread will catch on the hook surface. If the hook is not roughened, slippage can occur and the whole pattern will rotate on the hook when a peacock smashes it. Tie on the thread and drown everything in Super Glue to reinforce the fly's strength.

After you've made your first few wraps on the hook, add a drop of Super Glue to help secure the thread to the hook. The fly is 'built up' in stages. Start on the underside of the hook, tying in only one clump of short (usually red to simulate gills) bucktail. VeneKlasen notes that he ties in the bucktail with a collar for added strength (and not aesthetic beauty).

Step 5: Rotate the fly and tie in the tail section, always using a liberal amount of Super Glue. The top of the fly is then built up in stages of three or more clumps with plenty of Super Glue added in between clumps (this strengthens/secures the bucktail to the underlying material). Note that the underside of the fly should be very sparse in order for the pattern to swim upright.

Step 6: The largest prism eyes you can find are added at the very end of the tie. Use Devcon Five Minute Epoxy or one of the quick setting special no-poxy head glues, rotating the fly in the vise to get an even glue application. This final application not only enhances the fly's appearance, but also greatly increases its durability.

With the above details in mind, the fly fishing expert has come up with a simple pattern, called Garrett's Brycon/Amazon Annie, that even a novice tier can master. The fly is not only simple to tie, but quite fast to reproduce, according to VeneKlasen whose largest peacock was a 24 pounder that struck a red and yellow bucktail jig. He points out that you can go through a lot of flies in peacock country, so there's no sense in tying complicated recipes.

"I'll either fish the fly itself with a small slip sinker or tie the same pattern onto a small jig head," says the noted angler. "I use Kalin's jig heads because they have super-strong, wide-gap hooks. I fish it with a fast pulsating retrieve hold on for dear life."

VeneKlasen admits having very little success with trophy peacocks on the surface. This is not to say that a big peacock won't come up and take a fly off the surface, but huge poppers are exhausting to cast and strip for any length of time and streamers don't raise enough hell to bring a big fish out of deep water where they normally reside (unless they are feeding aggressively or spawning), according to the expert.

"With this in mind I use a stiff 9 or 10-weight rod, and a Cortland 325-Grain/24-foot sink tip Salmon-Steelhead Quick Descent line about 95 percent of the time," he says. "I don't like a full sink line because you often need to mend your running line if the boat drifts after you've made your cast. I don't kid around with leader material and neither should you. A 10-pound peacock will break 30-pound mono tippet with ease."

"It may sound like overkill, but I use a straight 6-foot piece of 50-pound Ande and still occasionally break off fish," VeneKlasen points out. "You'll need all the help you can get when that 20-pounder decides to take your streamer into a submerged tree. Tie the fly to the leader using an open-looped knot to enhance the fly's action."

"Forget the subtle twitch-and-let-sit largemouth method," he continues. "Anything twitched and floundered in the Amazon has long been extinct. Baitfish species that survive there have done so because of lightning speed and an ability to skate on water. A fast, erratic retrieve best imitates a panicked baitfish."

"Your retrieve can vary depending upon how aggressive the peacocks are," the expert fly fisherman advises. "Most of the time, I use a fast, 12-inch strip which starts with a quick snap of the wrist. This snapping action will drive even lethargic peacocks crazy. Slow your strip down for bedding fish or if the water is cold due to recent rains."

For those wanting to chat with VeneKlasen about his fly tying, catching or guided trips, contact him at InterAngler, P.O. Box 1171,

Tying Instructions for Peacock Deceivers

For those that want to tie up a few Peacock Deceivers at home, Dawn Smith offers the following guidance.

Step 1: Place hook, point up in your vise. Wrap thread onto hook going down shank 1/2". Tie in a bunch of white bucktail. Turn hook over in vise. Tie in colored bucktail. You can do combinations such as red and orange, orange and yellow, olive and gray, etc. Just keep the darkest color on top.

Step 2: Tie in pearl flash on sides, peacock flash on top and red flash on bottom. Your head should be large enough to support a medium prismatic eye.

Step 3: Stick on the eyes. Paint the Hard Head finish onto the head. Allow the finish to dry for 24 hours. The drying time seems excessive but this finish holds up better then head cement under onslaughts by peacock bass.

Angel Fire, NM 87710 or phone (888) 347-4329, or e-mail him at "interang@afweb.com".

"The Peacock Deceiver"

Expert fly casters Dawn and husband J.W. Smith have developed many Amazon peacock fly patterns, including their favorite, the Peacock Deceiver. Both have traveled and fished extensively in the Amazon region and in fact, J.W. is co-owner of Rod and Gun Resources, agent for several South American outfitters. On the Peacock Deceiver fly, J.W. caught three fish between 15 and 18 pounds on one March afternoon in 1998.

"While flyfishing usually produces many smaller fish, it can produce trophy-class fish as well," explains J.W. "Dawn and I do best on big peacocks by fishing the Peacock Deceiver deep, off points, tapered banks, submerged islands or in the middle of lagoons. We normally blind cast as the guide slowly moves the boat along."

"Trophy fish often travel in pairs," states Dawn, "so if you hook into one and are feeling generous, encourage your partner to cast in there with you. J. W. hooked a 33-inch peacock that we estimated at 22 pounds, and while he was fighting it, I cast my Peacock Deceiver repeatedly in the same area and quickly hooked and eventually landed a 35 1/2 inch fish that we estimated to be 25 pounds."

"They feed primarily on bait fish and slam into them in an attempt to stun or kill their prey before eating it," she continues. "Thus, the strike is often visible, even if the fish takes the fly two feet below the surface."

The Smiths believe that there is no stronger fish in the world on the initial strike and run than the peacock, so they have designed their 5- and 6-inch long Peacock Deceivers on Mustad 34011 stainless steel 3/0 or 4/0 hooks. They use a pre-waxed white monocord thread, peel-and-stick red medium-size prismatic eyes, pearl Krystal Flash on the sides. The wing is of peacock Krystal Flash and the beard of red Krystal Flash. The head finish is Loon Hard Head Fly Finish in white.

The body is formed with 5- to 6-inch long bucktail in red, orange, yellow, chartreuse, olive, gray and white. Fly color is largely dependent upon water clarity, according to the experts. Tannin water conditions in the Amazon call for bright colors like orange, chartreuse, red or yellow. Clear water conditions call for the above as well as olive variations. All color combinations should have white bellies, plenty of flash and red eyes, according to the Smiths.

"Although peacocks will take large topwater poppers, subsurface flies generally produce larger fish," says J.W. "We fish subsurface flies with a sink tip or sinking shooting head line on 8- to 10-weight flyrods."

"We prefer long casts with a three to five count hesitation after the fly hits the water before a medium to rapid retrieve," adds Dawn. "It is important to strip the flyline in close as strikes can occur within a few feet of the boat. If you miss the first strike, keep stripping because peacocks do not give up easily."

The Peacock Deceiver fly and other productive patterns can be ordered from Crystal's Fishing Critters, 3110 33rd Street, Lubbock, TX 79410 or phone (806) 793-2431. To chat fly fishing or trips with the Smiths, contact Rod and Gun Resources, 206 Ranch House Rd., Kerrville, TX 78028 or phone (800) 211-4753.

"Flash-Tail Whistler"

"Over the last 8 years fishing the upper Amazon with flies, I have had the best luck on Dan Blanton's Flash-Tail Whistler," notes Howard McKinney. "It's tied with a bushy red hackle and white bucktail with grizzly flanks. Lots of silver Flash-a-bou is tied to extend an inch beyond the bucktail. The fly should be tied as long as possible; 5 to 6 inches is ideal."

The same fly works well in Brazil in orange, yellow and gold with orange grizzly flank, according to the fly fisher. Lefty's Deceivers, white with green top and long Clouser Minnows also work great.

Another fly that is very productive in Amazon waters for McKinney is the rabbit strip streamer tied in a variety of colors.

"I always start with red and white," he says. "The nice thing about rabbit strip flies is that you can carry a small fly tying kit with a bunch of different colors of strips, some large bead chain for the eyes and a selection of hooks in a sandwich sized zip-lock bag. With this you can tie a variety of different color combos and sizes without having to bring a suitcase full of fly tying gear. This has saved my life on numerous occasions when the fish were hot on a particular color."

McKinney, who is a co-owner of the Fishabout agency, admits that working a fly rod popper for peacocks is a lot of work, but he contends that it pays off big time with explosive top-water strikes. He has had numerous productive days using large balsa poppers on 2/0 long shank hooks and also likes the new crystal poppers as well as Edgewater foam poppers.

"Throw the biggest popper you can handle," he suggests, "and work it back making as much noise on the surface as you can. The surface strikes will blow you right out of your shoes!"

Depending on conditions, McKinney recommends 3 different fly lines: a floater for poppers and shallow streamers, an intermediate or slow-sink like the Scientific Anglers Tarpon Taper for average streamer fishing in lagoons, and a fast sink Teeny Taper or Cortland Rapid Descent for fishing in rivers where there is current. The expert fishes 9 and 10 weight rods and lines to throw the large flies which are necessary to attract big peacocks.

"For leaders, I usually use either a straight shot of 50 pound test mono from the fly-line to the fly, or 50 pound with a 1 step taper to 30 pound between 6 and 8 feet," notes McKinney. "These fish are not the least bit leader shy. I tie all flies and poppers with a Lefty's non-slip loop knot to give the flies extra action when retrieved."

For comments on fly action or South American peacock bass opportunities, Howard McKinney can be contacted at Fishabout, P.O. Box 1679, Los Gatos, CA 95031 or phone (800) 409-2000.

"Ariramba Fly"

The Ariramba is a highly effective peacock bass fly developed by fly fishing expert, Rodolfo Fernandez of Montevideo, Uruguay. Working as a camp host for outfitter River Plate Anglers, he has spent many weeks chasing peacock bass in the Amazonas region of Brazil. Fernandez has employed his favorite fly primarily on three rivers in the Amazon Basin: the Matupiri, the Caures, and the Jufari (or Jauaperi).

*L*anding a big peacock on a fly rod can prove to be quite a task. Rodolfo Fernandez developed a noisy fly specifically for peacocks, like this one, in Amazon Basin waters.

He developed the fly over a two-month period after studying the waters, their color and depth and the minnows found inhabiting them. Fernandez, who ties the flies right on the river bank, named the Ariramba fly after the abundant kingfishers that fly all three waterways. Ariramba is a word in the dialect of the Indians that inhabit the Amazon Basin.

The hook used in the construction of the fly is a No. 3/0 Inox round bend, short or long shank, which is similar to many tarpon hooks. The Ariramba is constructed using natural colored buck tails. The fly's back is a dark gray or black, the lateral line is pink and light gray, and the belly is yellow. The head utilizes orange or red thread and the fly can be tied with or without eyes.

The key to the colorful fly's productivity may be the prominent back "hump." The Ariramba's hump creates more noise in the water and, is thus, more effective at attracting peacock bass.

"I've caught all four species of peacocks, the paca, barboleta, assu, and popoca, that we can find in the three rivers," notes Fernandez. "The Ariramba has taken both big and small peacocks, plus other species found in the Amazon Basin, such as jacunda, bicuda, and matrinxa. My largest peacock bass on the fly weighed about 19 pounds."

"I cast the fly with a No. 8 to 9 weight progressive rod with hard tip action," he explains. "I use either a No. 8 or 9 sinking or floating line. Floating works best in shallow waters of four feet or less and the sinking line is better in deeper waters."

Fernandez employs a clear gray, hard monofilament leader that is 2 feet long with his sinking line and one that is 7 feet long when he is using the floating line. The leader is 50 to 60 pound test and the reel has a line capacity of 80 yards of backing and No. 8 or 9 weight line.

"All of my peacock bass flies are developed in the same places that I am fishing," says the expert fly tier. "I thought the most appropriate name for this one is Ariramba, or kingfisher, in honor of the beautiful bird that inhabits the Amazon Basin. I dedicated this fly to a U.S. fisherman known for his great knowledge of those beautiful rivers in Brazil, Mr. Larry Larsen"

Such an acknowledgement makes me want to go out and catch some more peacocks on the Ariramba. While on a trip to the Rio Jufari, I personally witnessed the world-class fly fisher catch a giant butterfly peacock that would have weighed around 8 1/2 pounds on the very productive fly. I've only seen one significantly larger butterfly, and that was my all-tackle world record of 10 pounds, 8 ounces!

To talk fly fishing with Rodolfo Fernandez contact him at La Paz 2262, Montevideo, Uruguay or phone 011-05-982-400-3650 (fax 409-4740).

Optimal Success

While fly fishermen may miss some of the excitement of surface strikes by fishing streamers with sinking-tip lines, fly rodders may be a little more effective by utilizing a fly fishing-experienced camp manager or master guide/camp host. For optimal success, guides should be thoroughly drilled on fly fishing requisites, including correctly positioning the boat. Find an expert fly tier available in camp and the productivity should be maximized.

APPENDICES

APPENDIX I
"Peacock Bass Explosions" Contents

APPENDIX II
"Peacock Bass & Other Fierce Exotics" Contents

APPENDIX III
Outdoors Resource Directory

A good book on the species and fishing experience will provide detailed information on what to take along on the trip.

APPENDIX I

"Peacock Bass Explosions" Contents

Part 2. Preparing For Action

11. TOP TACTICS FOR TROPHIES
Trolling, school activating and other productive methods
Typical Haunts
Top Submergent and Surface Methods
Speed Trolling
School Activations
More Giant Doubles
Minnow-Bait Comeback

12. TACKLE FOR THE FRESHWATER BULLY
Here are the keys to productive lure selection
Topwater Plugs
Minnow Plugs
Searching The Depths
Jigs and Vibrating Plugs
Spoons and Spinners
Attention to Detail
Appropriate Tackle

13. FLYFISHING EXCITEMENT
Peacocks love to feed on the surface
Fly Class Records
Wading Action
Streamers and Poppers
Colors and Patterns
Cast-and-Retrieve Tactics
Outfitting For Location
Leader and Tippet Thoughts
Rod Weights
Stripping School

14. BOAT-SIDE BATTLES
The world's most explosive freshwater fish
Guide Overboard Maneuvers
Dumb, Mean and Powerful
Contact and Initial Run
Fight To Exhaustion

15. BIOLOGY AND LIFESTYLE
Behaviors are becoming to this brute
Sexual Maturity
Pre-Spawn Behavior
Spawning Behavior
Post-Spawn Behavior
Shared Parental Care
Juvenile Growth
Adult Growth
Foraging Preferences
Bass Feeding Comparisons
Foreign Competition
Survival of The Fittest

16. TRAVEL TIPS/REQUIREMENTS
Health, Timing, Equipment and Expectations
Travel Requirements/Options
Health Precautions
Clothing and Personal Items
Packing Tips and Tricks
Timing Your Venture
The Right Equipment For Handling Peacocks
Other Fishing Tackle You'll Need
The Guides, Language And Tipping

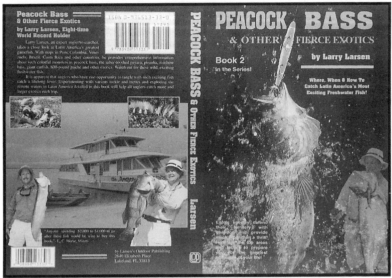

*M*ore information on the greatest fish on earth and a few other exciting species that live in the same waters as the peacock.

APPENDIX II

"Peacock Bass & Other Fierce Exotics" Contents
INTRODUCTION - THE FIERCE EXOTICS ON TRIAL

1. **BLACK RIVER YACHTING FOR GIANTS**
   Check out the Amazon's long, twisting "roadway" in comfort
   Jungle River Fertility
   Doubling Up On The "Schoolers"
   Rio Negro Rock Obstacles
   Nature's Botanical Garden
   Igapos, Paranas & Furos
   Archipelago Islands & Peacocks
   Release - A Foreign Concept
2. **PERUVIAN HEADWATERS GOLD**
   Peru's sporty peacocks will smash every lure in the tackle box
   Consistent Strikes and Catches
   The Line On Lagoon Peacocks
   Vivid, Weird Characteristics
   Economy and Comfort
   Native Net Pressure
   Land-Locked Lagoon Action
   New and Other Options
3. **SAFARI CAMP PEACOCKS IN THE RAINFOREST**
   Battle the giant 3-bar peacock and monster butterflies
   The Jungle Awakes
   Skinny Lagoons & Fat Peacocks
   Focus On The Bocas
   Roll Casts On The Fly
   Camp Comfort
   The Primitive Outback
   Giant Butterfly Peacock
4. **JUNGLE RIVERBOAT TUCUNARE**
   Explore the Brazilian rainforest rivers of Uatuma and Jatupu
   Exploring The Uatuma Watershed
   Giants, Numbers and Variety
   Oxbows and False Channels Galore
   Dolphin Foraging Reaction
   Territorial and Feeding Strikes
   Piranha Myths and Lore
5. **VENEZUELA OUTBACK TREASURES**
   Try the options: monster grande pavon, royal peacocks & payara
   Maintaining A Healthy Fishery
   Pasimoni and Pasiba Excitement
   The Ventuari's Rocky, Brown Islands
   Scurrying Bait & Fatal Attractions
   Cinaruco River Studies
   Monseratt Mysteries

PEACOCK BASS SERIES by Larry Larsen

(PF1) PEACOCK BASS EXPLOSIONS! - A must read for those anglers who are interested in catching the world's most exciting fresh water fish! Detailed tips, trip planning and tactics for peacocks in South Florida, Venezuela, Brazil, Puerto Rico, Hawaii and other destinations. This book explores the most effective tactics to take the aggressive peacock bass. Invaluable to all adventurous anglers!

(PF2) PEACOCK BASS & OTHER FIERCE EXOTICS - Book 2 in the Series reveals the latest techniques and best spots to prepare you for the greatest fishing experience of your life! You'll learn how to catch more and larger fish using the valuable information from the author and expert angler, a seven-time peacock bass world-record holder. It's the first comprehensive discussion on this wild and colorful fish. With stops in Peru, Colombia, Venezuela and Brazil, he provides information about colorful monster payara, and other exotic fish.

(PF3) PEACOCK BASS ADDICTION - Book 3 in the Series focuses on catching America's greatest gamefish, the peacock bass. It offers tips on where, when and how to catch this exciting fish, including range/seasonal movements, fly fishing tips, battle tips and top locations in the world. Comprehensive tackle/equipment recommendations and Larry's secrets to finding the most productive habitats within the most productive lagoons to catch giant peacock bass are presented.

BASS WATERS GUIDE SERIES by Larry Larsen

(BW2) GUIDE TO CENTRAL FLORIDA BASS WATERS - Covers from Tampa/Orlando to Palatka. Includes Lakes George, Rodman, Monroe, Tarpon and the Harris Chain, the St. Johns, Oklawaha and Withlacoochee Rivers, the Ocala Forest, Crystal River, Hillsborough River, Conway Chain, Homosassa River, Lake Minneola, Lake Weir, Lake Hart, Spring Runs and many more!

> **TATTERED BOOKS!**
> *"The Bass Waters Series are as great as the rest of your bass books. I must have read the Central FL book 50 times!" R. Michalski, Meridien, CT*

(BW3) GUIDE TO SOUTH FLORIDA BASS WATERS - Covers from I-4 to the Everglades. Includes Lakes Toho, Kissimmee, Okeechobee, Poinsett, Tenoroc, Blue Cypress, the Winter Haven Chain, Fellsmere Farm 13, Caloosahatchee River, Lake June-in-Winter, the Everglades, Lake Istokpoga, Peace River, Crooked Lake, Lake Osborne, St. Lucie Canal, Shell Creek, Lake Marian, Lake Pierce, Web Lake and many other popular overlooked waters.

SALTWATER FISHING GUIDES by Frank Sargeant

A unique "where-to" series of detailed secret spots; hundreds of little-known honeyholes and exactly how to fish them. Prime seasons, baits and lures, marinas and dozens of detailed maps are included. The comprehensive index helps the reader to further pinpoint productive areas and tactics. Over $160 worth of personally-marked NOAA charts.

(FG1) FRANK SARGEANT'S SECRET SPOTS Tampa Bay to Cedar Key - Covers Hillsborough River and Davis Island through the Manatee River, Mullet Key and the Suwannee River.

(FG2) FRANK SARGEANT'S SECRET SPOTS Southwest Florida Covers from Sarasota Bay to Marco.

INSHORE SERIES by Frank Sargeant

(IL1) THE SNOOK BOOK-Every aspect of finding and catching big snook, in all seasons and all waters where they are found.

(IL2) THE REDFISH BOOK- Secret techniques are revealed for the first time. After reading this informative book, you'll catch more redfish on your next trip!

> **EXCELLENT PUBLICATIONS!**
> *"I would like to commend Frank on his excellent saltwater fishing series. I own them all and have read each of them three or four times!"*
> W. La Piedra, Cape Coral, FL

(IL3) THE TARPON BOOK-Find and catch the wily "silver king" along the Gulf Coast, north through the mid-Atlantic, and south along Central and South American coastlines.

(IL4) THE TROUT BOOK -Jammed with tips for both the old salt and the rank amateur who pursue the spotted weakfish, or seatrout, throughout the coastal waters of the Gulf and Atlantic.

SALTWATER SERIES by Frank Sargeant

(SW1) THE REEF FISHING BOOK - An all-in-one compilation of the best techniques, lures and locations for grouper and snapper and other reef species, including how to find and catch live bait, trolling techniques and the latest rod and reels for success. Special features include where the biggest fish live, electronics savvy, anchoring tricks and much more!

(SW1) MASTERS BOOK OF SNOOK - Secrets of top professional skippers for finding giant snook year around. Includes tips for mastering the tides, live baiting, nighttime fishing and more.

HUNTING LIBRARY by John E. Phillips

(DH1) MASTERS' SECRETS OF DEER HUNTING - New tactics and strategies, the most comprehensive book of its kind.

(DH2) THE SCIENCE OF DEER HUNTING Covers many of the toughest deer hunting problems a sportsman ever encounters!

(DH3) MASTERS' SECRETS OF BOW-HUNTING DEER - Special skills are required to take more bucks with a bow, even during gun season.

> **RECOMMENDATION!**
> *"The Masters' Secrets series are some of the best books around."* - *J.Spencer, Stuttgart, AR*

(DH4) HOW TO TAKE MONSTER BUCKS -Specific techniques that will almost guarantee a trophy buck next season!

(TH1) MASTERS' SECRETS OF TURKEY HUNTING - Avoid the 10 deadly sins of turkey hunting.

FISHING LIBRARY

(CF1) MASTERS' SECRETS OF CRAPPIE FISHING by John E. Phillips   Learn how to make crappie start biting again once they have stopped, in any type of weather.

(CF2) CRAPPIE TACTICS by Larry Larsen - This book will improve your catch! The book includes some basics for fun fishing, advanced techniques for year 'round crappie and tournament preparation.

(CF3) MASTERS' SECRETS OF CATFISHING by John E. Phillips Your best guide to catching the best-tasting, elusive cats. Learn the best time of the year, the most productive places and which states to fish.

TRAVEL / DIVING / NATURE BOOKS

(OT3) FISH & DIVE FLORIDA & The Keys - by M. Timothy O'Keefe & Larry Larsen - Where and how to plan a vacation to America's most popular fishing and diving destination.

(DL2) MANATEES - OUR VANISHING MERMAIDS - An in-depth overview of nature's strangest-looking, mos endangered mammals. Dive with manatees, why they may be living fossils, their unique life cycle, and much more.

(DL3) SEA TURTLES - THE WATCHERS' GUIDE - Discover Florida's sea turtle nesting sites. Provides the specifics of appropriate personal conduct and behavior for human beings on turtle nesting beaches.

QUALITY PEACOCK BASS T-SHIRTS

The beautiful paintings on the cover of "Peacock Bass Addiction" and on the back cover of "Peacock Bass Explosions" are available on all-cotton T-Shirts. These quality white shirts with art on the front can be ordered in M, L or XL.

TS-1- Peacock Bass Explosions ... $19.00

TS-2- Peacock Bass Addiction ... $19.00

TEAM T-SHIRT (wearing TS-1), catches more peacock bass!

LIMITED EDITION PRINTS

Limited Edition Prints of our beautiful paintings individually numbered and personally signed by the artists are also available. The collector's items are suitable for framing and decorative for any room in the house or office.

LEP-1 - Peacock Bass Explosions ... $48.00

LEP-2 - Peacock Bass Addiction ... $48.00

TO ORDER: mail check with this order form to Larry Larsen, LOP, 2640 Elizabeth Place, Lakeland, FL 33813

____ # TS1	(Size M L XL) @ $19 each	= _____
____ # TS2	(Size M L XL) @ $19 each	= _____
____ # LEP 1	@$48 each	= _____
____ # LEP 2	@$48 each	= _____

(prices include shipping/handling. Add $2 per item for priority mail)

Name_____

Address_____   **Total**

City/State/Zip_____   **Enclosed $_____**

LARSEN'S OUTDOOR PUBLISHING
CONVENIENT ORDER FORM
ALL PRICES INCLUDE POSTAGE/HANDLING

FRESH WATER

___ BSL3. Bass Pro Strategies ($14.95)
___ BSL4. Bass Lures/Tech. ($14.95)
___ BSL5. Shallow Water Bass ($14.95)
___ BSL6. Bass Fishing Facts ($13.95)
___ BSL8. Bass Patterns ($14.95)
___ BSL9. Bass Guide Tips ($14.95)
___ CF1. Mstrs' Scrts/Crappie Fshg ($12.95)
___ CF2. Crappie Tactics ($12.95)
___ CF3. Mstr's Secrets of Catfishing ($12.95)
___ LB1. Larsen on Bass Tactics ($15.95)
___ PF1. Peacock Bass Explosions! ($16.95)
___ PF2. Peacock Bass & Other Fierce
           Exotics ($17.95)
___ PF3. Peacock Bass Addiction ($18.95)

SALT WATER

___ IL1. The Snook Book   ($14.95)
___ IL2. The Redfish Book ($14.95)
___ IL3. The Tarpon Book ($14.95)
___ IL4. The Trout Book ($14.95)
___ SW1. The Reef Fishing Book ($16.45)
___ SW2. Masters Bk/Snook ($16.45)

REGIONAL

___ FG1. Secret Spots-Tampa Bay/
           Cedar Key   ($15.95)
___ FG2. Secret Spots - SW Florida ($15.95)
___ BW1. Guide/North Fl. Waters ($16.95)
___ BW2. Guide/Cntral Fl.Waters ($15.95)
___ BW3. Guide/South Fl.Waters ($15.95)
___ OT3. Fish/Dive Florida/ Keys ($13.95)

HUNTING

___ DH1. Mstrs' Secrets/ Deer Hunting ($14.95)
___ DH2. Science of Deer Hunting ($14.95)
___ DH3. Mstrs' Secrets/Bowhunting ($12.45)
___ DH4. How to Take Monster Bucks ($13.95)
___ TH1. Mstrs' Secrets/ Turkey Hunting ($14.95)

OTHER OUTDOORS BOOKS

___ DL2. Manatees/Vanishing ($11.45)
___ DL3. Sea Turtles/Watchers' ($11.45)

FREE BROCHURES

___ Peacock Bass Brochure
___ LOP Book Catalog

BIG MULTI-BOOK DISCOUNT!
2-3 books, SAVE 10%
4 or more books, SAVE 20%

INTERNATIONAL AIRMAIL ORDERS
Send check in U.S. funds; add $6 more for 1 book, $4 for each additional book

---

ALL PRICES INCLUDE U.S. POSTAGE/HANDLING

No. of books _____ x $_____ ea   = $_____
No. of books _____ x $_____ ea   = $_____
   Multi-book Discount   (%) $_____
SUBTOTAL $_____

☐ **Priority Mail (add $2.50 more for every 2 books)** $_____
   TOTAL ENCLOSED (check or money order) $_____

NAME_____ ADDRESS_____

CITY_____ STATE_____ ZIP_____

**Send check/Money Order to: Larsen's Outdoor Publishing,
Dept. BR99, 2640 Elizabeth Place, Lakeland, FL 33813**
(Sorry, no credit card orders)

INDEX

Symbols

A

B

C

ABOUT OUR FRONT COVER AND THE ARTIST

George Liska of Pisces Portraits is an accomplished artist, illustrator and raconteur based in Orlando, Florida. He does "unique fine art of your special fish", and we highly recommend his work. His outstanding painting is shown on the cover of "Peacock Bass Addiction". He has painted numerous exotic species from around the world and has won many awards for such. For a great Limited Edition Print of our cover, see page 182. To commission a painting of any species of fish, contact him at 4328 Edgewater Dr., Apt. C-201, Orlando, FL 32804 or phone 407/293-6411.